# *Making it Easy*
# Cajun Cooking

## Recipes and Remembrances from Acadiana

### Arlene Coco

**Library of Congress Cataloging-in-Publication Data**

Coco, Arlene.
  Making it easy : Cajun cooking / Arlene Coco.
      p.  cm.
  ISBN  1-55622-649-7 (pbk.)
  1.  Cookery, American—Louisiana style.   2.  Cookery,
Cajun.   I.  Title.
  TX715.2.L68C63      1998
  641.59763—dc21                            98-34441
                                            CIP

© 1999, Arlene Coco
All Rights Reserved

Printed in the United States of America

ISBN 1-55622-649-7
10 9 8 7 6 5 4 3 2 1
9810

All inquiries for volume purchases of this book should be addressed to Wordware Publishing, Inc., at 2320 Los Rios Boulevard,
Plano, Texas 75074. Telephone inquiries may be made by calling:
                          (972) 423-0090

# Dedication

To my mother, who took the time to inspire me and taught me that any dream is possible.

# Acknowledgments

Writing a book requires a tremendous amount of work from lots of people. I would like to express my thanks to everyone who has helped me with this book. I must start by thanking my husband, Martin, whose patience and understanding is never ending. He holds the important position in my company as "quality control," which can be a daunting job at times. Martin also took care of the vegetable garden, which made the dishes taste delicious and remarkable.

A special thanks goes to my mother, who has helped me gather the family recipes, and my brother Warren and his wife, Donna, who spent the time teaching me the techniques and finer points of cooking wild game.

The staff at Republic of Texas Press, especially Ginnie Bivona, gave me guidance when I needed it most. Ginnie helped me make this dream a reality.

My thanks also to Bonnie Koepp, who took great care with the details and editing.

Also, to my friend Donald James, who has always been there when I needed another chef to check reality.

Writing about something I love is a privilege, and none of it would happen without the support of my dear friends and customers. Thank you most of all.

# List of Recipes

## Salads

## Mama's Cajun Sideboard

## Desserts

# Beverages

# Introduction

Growing up in the country always gave me a sense of peacefulness. I had a childhood filled with long, hot summer days playing by the creeks and bayous of South Louisiana.

I think when we get older we always try to re-create the atmosphere in which we grew up. We do this by rituals at holidays and passing on the stories and culture to our children.

In this book, I share some of those rituals and pass along some of our family folklore and history.

Some of the recipes are for special occasions and take a little more time, but most are do-ahead, easy, and freeze very well. Cajun food always tastes better the next day because it gives a chance for the flavors to "marry" and time for the cook to rest.

This book is the story of my culinary odyssey, from the days when life was simple and the living was easy.

# Lagniappe, or Chef's Secrets

Lagniappe is an old Cajun term that means "a little something extra," a treat, if you will, or something for free.

Over the past twenty years or so, I have picked up a few ideas that have stood the test of time. When I travel or take classes, I only try to take away one idea and use it in my cooking. The key to successful cooking is to be organized, but don't forget the most important ingredient in any recipe is to have fun! I would like to share some "one-liners" that I have learned from other chefs that have made life in the kitchen a little easier.

- It is easier to grate or "zest" citrus rinds that have been frozen first. Also, putting a piece of plastic wrap on the grater over the holes makes the job easier because the zest sticks to the plastic. Pull the plastic off the grater and the zest is easily collected.

- For soup stock rich with flavor and color, brown the bones, carrots, and onions under the broiler.

- Peel garlic easily by chopping off the ends and hitting the clove with the back of a knife on a cutting board.

- Forming meatballs is easier if hands are first chilled with ice.

- To remove the "slime" when cooking okra, add a dash of vinegar.

- Raw mushrooms, kiwi, and strawberries can be sliced evenly and quickly with an egg slicer, and egg salad can be made as well by placing the egg the opposite way on the slicer for a second slice.

- To cut fresh bread, heat a serrated knife for 10 seconds over a low flame.

- For even slices when cutting bread, salami, etc., keep your eye on the large portion when slicing; this will keep your focus in perspective.

- Cheese can be sliced thinner with a dull knife because of the fat content.

- To keep sliced, halved, or mashed avocado from turning brown, always put the seed on top and refrigerate until served; then root the seed in a glass of water.

- Cream butter and sugar together more quickly by adding a little cream in the mixing bowl.

- Shave chocolate with a potato peeler for thin curls, then freeze until needed.

- To keep mold off cheese, first wipe with vinegar and then put two lumps of sugar with the cheese in an airtight container. Store cheese at 40°F for the best flavor.

- A sugar cube in olive oil keeps it from becoming spoiled.

- Because metal is such a good heat conductor, bake potatoes with small metal skewers inserted to shorten cooking time.

- To stop bacon and hamburger from spattering, sprinkle water in the cold frying pan before cooking.

- When cooking tougher cuts of meat, add a small amount of lime juice to the pot for tenderizing.

- Put lemon on fish after cooking, never before, to keep it from getting mushy.

- Soak frozen fish in milk to give it that fresh-caught flavor. Drain before cooking.

- If soups or stews are too salty, add a few slices of potato, boil a few minutes, and remove. If that does not work, add a teaspoon of sugar.

- Curdled hollandaise sauce can be saved by mixing one more egg yolk with a little melted butter and stirring it into the sauce, then adding a little hot water.

- Before peeling peaches, cover with boiling water and let stand for five minutes; drain and cover with plastic wrap. The skin can then be removed easily.

- To clean pecan meats from the shell easily, freeze for three days and crack while frozen.

- Keep coffee in your freezer for better flavor.

- For a quick and healthy alternative thickener for soups, combine cooked vegetables such as potatoes, onions, and carrots in a blender; or in a pinch, use instant mashed potatoes.

- Store peeled garlic cloves in a jar filled with olive oil and herbs in the refrigerator; use the oil for cooking.

- For fresh flavor in orange juice, add the juice of a lime.

- To make pot roast or stewing meat tender, use two cups of hot tea or coffee as a cooking liquid.

- To cut boiled eggs neatly, use a knife rinsed in hot water, and remember to only simmer eggs for 13 minutes; there is no need to boil them rapidly.

- Brush tamari sauce on meat before broiling for a rich, brown color.

- To keep boiled potatoes white, add a teaspoon of lime juice or rice vinegar to the water.

- To grind nuts quickly, crush them with a rolling pin or wooden mallet between sheets of plastic wrap.

- To soften cold butter, slice into a warm bowl, or if it is frozen, grate it on plastic wrap.

- Store Portobello mushrooms in a paper bag to absorb moisture and keep flavor.

- Write the date on everything when storing in the freezer so older items can be used first.

- To freeze foods like berries and appetizers for easy separation, first spread out on a cookie sheet until frozen and then pack in plastic bags with the date on them.

- Add salt to pasta water; this will raise the temperature and food will cook quicker.

- A slow rolling boil cooks as quickly as a fast boil. It also reduces heat and humidity in the kitchen.

- To keep parsley fresh rinse chopped parsley in a thin cotton towel, squeeze dry, place in a dry screw-top container, and refrigerate.

- Put a dry sponge in the vegetable crisper drawer of refrigerator to absorb moisture; to kill germs in that sponge, place it in the microwave for one minute.

- Always wash cutting boards between items to prevent cross contamination.

- To dry lots of lettuce or spinach for a party, put in a pillowcase, tie with twist tie, and swing!

- To crisp celery, place in a pan of cold water with a slices of raw potato. Let stand for a few hours, then drain. Radishes work also with this method.

- Keep ready-to-use whipped cream on hand. Whip one pint whipping cream with four tablespoons of sugar. Drop in peaks on a cookie sheet to freeze. Sprinkle with powdered sugar; transfer to airtight containers and store in freezer. Remove 15 minutes before serving to thaw.

- To reheat dry bread, put it in a wet brown paper bag in a 200°F oven.

- When removing a small amount of eggshell from a bowl, use a half eggshell as a scoop.

- To season wooden cutting boards and bowls, rub with olive oil. Leave overnight and buff with a soft cloth.

- A stove fire can be extinguished quickly by dumping baking soda on the flame.

- To prevent scratching of Teflon pans, place a paper towel in between them when storing.

- Fruits and vegetables ripen faster when placed in a paper bag.

- Let egg whites warm to room temperature before beating for greater volume; remember to use a clean whisk and bowl.

- For the best flavors in salad dressings, mix the spice seasoning with vinegar before adding the oil.

- Rice will be fluffier and drier if crackers are put on top of it after cooking.

- Season salads, deviled eggs, salad dressings, etc., with pickled jalapeño juice.

- A slice of lime in a bottle of olives will make them taste fresher.

- Add apple juice concentrate to pancake batter for more flavor.

- Heavy molasses and honey are less apt to stick if you coat the measuring cup with a little oil.

- While cooking vegetables, avoid odors by adding a slice of bread; it will pour off with the water.

- Let dough rise in a zip-close bag; it can be punched down and kneaded without drying out.

- Use a tomato corer to remove stems from strawberries.

- Do not keep dry herbs more than six months; they lose strength after that.

# The Basics

In every type of ethnic cuisine there are basic recipes and techniques that everyone follows. These recipes and ideas are typically handed down through the generations, and not much is written down. And if they are written down, something is always left out. To continue to preserve family culture, cooking together is a great way to document the recipes.

In my family, we try to share recipes and techniques every time we get together. In all of my travels and discussions, I have realized that there are certain things that never change about Cajun cooking, regardless of origin, and I put them under the category of "my mama told me."

- The "holy trinity" makes up a majority of the dishes—green or "bell pepper," celery, and onion.

- Garlic is liberally used, since Louisiana is a major garlic producer for the United States.

- A roux is the base of many Cajun dishes.

- Black iron skillets and pots, well worn and seasoned, make the best cooking vessels.

- Green onions and parsley chopped fresh always get stirred in at the end of the dish right before serving.

- Cajun food is not "burn your mouth off" hot. The hot sauce is usually on the table.

- Long grain or converted rice is best for cooking Cajun food. It absorbs flavors very well.

- Spice blends are used to add a special touch. Every Cajun cook has her own personal house blend that she uses as a "secret weapon."

- Kosher salt does not break down foods; this is especially good when preparing cold foods.

# Roux 101

The very word roux can be confusing, let alone making it and adding it to something else. When I was very young I spent a lot of time with my mother because we lived in a rural area. I would watch her endlessly stir at the stove. Then after a while, I would smell that familiar nutty smell and I knew that meant something tasty for supper that night. I particularly remember in the winter when the heat from the kitchen used to steam the windows in the kitchen. It's funny what sticks in your mind over the years about your childhood. When I visit Louisiana, my mother still makes my favorite homecoming dishes—almost all starting with a roux.

Times have changed in Louisiana when it comes to roux. On a recent visit through the heart of Cajun country I discovered in a small meat market a product called "dry roux." After interrogating the local cooks, it came to me that this was a wonderful thing because it made all of the flavor possible without the fat. Yes, a fat-free roux! I had heard of this technique years before, but now it is mainstream for the local cooks for two reasons—convenience and health.

# Dry Roux

Yields approximately 2 cups

### Ingredients

2   cups flour
Pinch of salt
Pinch of sugar

**Stove top**

In a black iron skillet with a wooden spoon, mix all ingredients and stir over medium low heat. After about 20 minutes, flour will start to lose moisture and turn darker. When dark, remove from heat and cool. Store in the refrigerator.

*Chef's secret:* To substitute dry for wet roux in a recipe, the following techniques can be used:

*Melt the original amount of butter in the recipe and sauté the vegetables in it; add the same amount of dry roux after the vegetables are soft.*

*For a fat-free roux, spray a non-stick pan with oil and sauté vegetables until soft, omitting the butter. When soft, add the dry roux and liquid as usual.*

❧ Dry roux keeps in the refrigerator about two weeks in a sealed container.

# Original Cajun Roux

Yields 1 cup

### Ingredients

½  cup flour
½  cup butter, oil, or margarine

**Stove top**

In a black iron skillet with a wooden spoon (long handled, please), melt butter and add flour, stirring over medium low heat, until you have the color of roux you want. Be patient . . . making a roux is a spiritual experience!

It's a good idea to make a large batch and keep it on hand when you are feeling a little Cajun.

As a general rule, a roux is made with half fat and half flour.

There are different types of roux:

- A blond roux is cooked just enough to have a little color and the flour taste cooked out. This is used for cream sauces and light poultry sauces.

- A brown roux is a little darker and used for stews and heavier dishes.

- A dark brown roux is even darker and is used for gumbos and wild game dishes.

My suggestion is to practice making a roux if you have never made one. Do it on a day when you can make it without interruptions. Once you start, you cannot leave the stirring process. It is not a difficult process; it just takes patience. If you cook it on too high of a heat and black flecks start to appear, that means it has burned and you will have to throw it out and start over. This type of roux keeps in the refrigerator for up to a week.

# Seasoning Blends

Any cook worth his salt in Louisiana has the ability to season. It is a talent most are taught at a young age. I was always in charge of picking herbs and vegetables for the day from the garden. This always included fresh parsley and green onions and any other ideas my mama had for that day. Although seasoning blends are a modern-day creation, for convenience they hold an important place in today's Cajun cuisine.

When creating your own seasoning blend, you must consider such things as salt or no salt; sugar or no sugar; is it a standard for everyday cooking, or is it for special dishes only?

The recipes on the following pages are two standard blends that can add zip to just about anything except bread pudding!

# Cajun Sensation Spice Blend

Yields approximately ½ cup

### Ingredients

| | |
|---|---|
| 1 | tablespoon paprika |
| 1 | teaspoon kosher salt |
| 1 | teaspoon black pepper |
| 1 | teaspoon red or cayenne pepper |
| 1 | teaspoon garlic powder |
| 1 | teaspoon onion powder |
| 1 | teaspoon dried basil leaves |
| 1 | teaspoon dried marjoram leaves |
| 1 | teaspoon dried mustard |
| 1 | teaspoon sugar (optional) |

No cooking

Mix together and store in an airtight container.

# Cajun Sass Seasoning Blend

Yields approximately ⅓ cup

This one is a little flakier and hotter.

### Ingredients

| | |
|---|---|
| 2 | tablespoons minced dried onion flakes |
| 2 | tablespoons dried parsley |
| 1 | tablespoon minced dried garlic |
| 1 | tablespoon dried red pepper flakes |

No cooking

Mix together and store in an airtight container.

# Cajun Cream Sauce

Makes 4 cups

## Ingredients

2 cups half-and-half
½ cup dry roux
Pinch nutmeg
1 teaspoon Cajun Sensation Spice Blend (page 10)

Stove top

Heat half-and-half. Whisk in dry roux and simmer until thickened. Add nutmeg and spice blend. Simmer on low heat until thick. Strain if needed.

# Breakfast and Brunches

One cannot think of entertaining in Louisiana without including food. With their hospitable nature, cooks from the Bayou State are devoted to creating specialties of the house, and they have endless discussions, sometimes quite heated, about whose recipe for a certain dish is the authentic one. Great care is taken in choosing the right ingredients, and sincere love and kindness are important additions to any dish.

If there ever was a food creed in New Orleans, brunch is it. It is the backbone of relaxed entertaining. Traditionally, families gathered after church for a meal. Each family brought a dish created from what was in season at that time. This was a time to visit with kin, eat great food, and play. Today, brunch most often starts at noon or even later, the key being dishes prepared in advance that hold well and can be served easily.

Brunch is customarily started with a spicy beverage like a Bloody Mary or something smooth and creamy like a Brandy Alexander, followed by an appetizer or breakfast bread, depending on the time of day. Earlier parties seem to have more egg dishes for entrees, and later brunches lean more towards a heavier fare such as my favorite, grillades.

The most important thing to remember about brunches is that the atmosphere should be relaxed. Decorate with balloons and place fresh flowers on the buffet trays. Your guests will think you were up all night getting ready!

The following recipe is one of my most popular brunch dishes. It can be prepared the night before and baked the next morning. Any recipe that can be prepared in advance gets extra marks in my book! The ingredients that can be used are only limited by one's own imagination.

# Opelousas Potato Pie

Yields 8-10 servings

*This dish was a specialty of my Uncle Paul's. I will always remember going to his house on Saturdays because it was one of my favorite places. He had a fig orchard in his backyard, which was prime climbing. All of the kids used to help with the gardening chores, and afterwards, he would make us this pie for lunch.*

## Ingredients

| | |
|---|---|
| 1 | 1-pound bag frozen southern hash brown potatoes |
| 1 | tablespoon butter |
| 1 | large onion, chopped |
| 1 | pound diced ham or cooked sausage, crumbled |
| 2 | 10-ounce packages chopped spinach, thawed and drained |
| 8 | large eggs |
| 1 | quart half-and-half cream |
| 1 | 10-ounce can cream of mushroom soup |
| 1 | tablespoon Worcestershire sauce |
| 1 | teaspoon hot sauce |
| ⅛ | teaspoon grated nutmeg |
| 2 | teaspoons kosher salt |
| ½ | teaspoon black pepper |
| 2 | cups cheddar cheese, shredded |
| 3 | tablespoons parsley, chopped |
| 3 | tablespoons sweet red pepper, chopped |

Preheat oven to 350°F

**1.** Place potatoes in a three-quart casserole dish. Roast in oven at 350°F for 30 minutes until slightly browned.

**2.** Over medium heat, melt butter and sauté onion and ham for 5 minutes or until onions become soft. Spoon mixture over potatoes.

**3.** Squeeze the water thoroughly from the spinach and layer over mixture.

**4.** Beat eggs, cream, and soup together until blended. Add all seasonings except parsley and red pepper.

**5.** Pour over mixture and sprinkle cheese on top. Cover with plastic wrap and refrigerate overnight.

**6.** Bake in a preheated 350ºF oven for 1 hour. Let stand for 10 minutes before serving and sprinkle with chopped parsley and sweet red pepper.

**To serve:** It can also be served at room temperature.

## Shopping List

| | |
|---|---|
| frozen hash browns | Worcestershire sauce |
| butter | Louisiana hot sauce |
| diced ham or cooked sausage | nutmeg |
| large onion | kosher salt |
| frozen spinach | black pepper |
| half-and-half cream | cheddar cheese |
| canned cream of mushroom soup | parsley |
| eggs | sweet red pepper |

***Chef's secret:*** *This dish freezes well. Prepare through step 5. To cook, thaw by placing the dish in the refrigerator the day before it is to be served. On the big day, finish with step 6.*

**Tip:** You can freeze leftover chopped red pepper for another use.

# Spicy Shrimp and Andouille Crepes

### Serves 6

*A*ndouille sausage is a spicy pork sausage that goes well with many Cajun flavors. The delicate crepes are a perfect holder for this bold filling. During my restaurant days in New Orleans, we served crepes every day.

## Ingredients

**Crepe Batter:**
- ½ cup flour
- ½ cup milk
- ¼ cup warm water
- 2 large eggs
- 2 tablespoons butter, melted
- 1 teaspoon Cajun Sensation Spice Blend (page 10)
- Unsalted butter for frying

**Filling:**
- 1 pound Andouille sausage, sliced
- 1 large onion, chopped
- 1 large green or red pepper, chopped
- 3 ribs of celery, chopped
- 1 tablespoon garlic, minced
- 8 ounces sliced mushrooms
- 1 15-ounce can diced tomatoes, drained
- ½ cup fresh basil, chopped
- 1 pound shelled shrimp, cooked and chopped in large pieces
- 2 teaspoons Cajun Sass Seasoning Blend (page 11)
- 1 teaspoon brown sugar
- 1 teaspoon kosher salt
- ½ teaspoon liquid smoke
- 2 cups mozzarella cheese, shredded
- ½ bunch green onions, sliced

## Directions for Crepe Batter:

**1.** Combine flour, milk, water, eggs, and melted butter in a blender until smooth.

**2.** Pour the batter in a pitcher and let rest for 30 minutes. (Batter can be made up to one day in advance.)

**3.** In a non-stick pan, melt a little butter and coat the pan. Pour about 2 tablespoons of batter in the pan and swirl until a thin layer covers the pan.

**4.** Cook about 2 minutes or until the bottom is brown. Flip over and brown the other side slightly.

**5.** Butter the pan before cooking each crepe. Stack with parchment paper or plastic wrap between each layer.

Preheat oven to 350°F

**Directions for Filling:**

**1.** In a large skillet, sauté sausage for 5 minutes on medium heat. Remove from pan and keep warm.

**2.** Sauté onion, pepper, celery, garlic, and mushrooms for 5 minutes or until soft.

**3.** Add tomatoes, basil, shrimp, Cajun spice, sugar, salt, and liquid smoke. Simmer on low heat until warm, about 10 minutes. Add sausage and cook another 20 minutes. Let cool.

**4.** With a slotted spoon, fill crepes with warm filling, roll up, place in baking pans, and top with shredded cheese.

**5.** Heat in 350°F oven for 10 minutes and lower to 200°F to keep warm until serving time.

**To serve:** Sprinkle with sliced green onion and serve with fresh sliced fruit garnished with fresh mint.

*Chef's secret: Smoked turkey sausage can be substituted for Andouille sausage.*

### Shopping List

- all-purpose flour
- milk
- eggs
- butter, unsalted
- Cajun Sensation Spice Blend
- Andouille sausage
- large onion
- green or red pepper
- celery
- garlic
- mushrooms
- canned diced tomatoes
- fresh basil
- shelled shrimp, cooked and chopped in large pieces
- Cajun Sass Seasoning Blend
- brown sugar
- kosher salt
- liquid smoke
- green onions
- shredded mozzarella cheese

# Apple Pecan Praline French Toast Bake

Serves 8-10

*F*rench toast has another name in Louisiana: It's often referred to as "Pain Perdu," which means lost bread. That is what would happen to the bread if you did not use it up. This is an updated version of that dish with apples and nuts to jazz it up.

## Ingredients

**French Toast:**

1    large French bread loaf, sliced
8    large eggs
1    quart half-and-half cream
1    teaspoon almond extract
½    teaspoon ground cinnamon
½    teaspoon ground nutmeg
Pinch of salt

**Apple Pecan Praline Topping:**

3    apples, peeled and grated on large side of grater
2    sticks (1 cup) butter, softened
1    cup packed dark brown sugar
1    cup chopped pecans
½    teaspoon ground cinnamon
½    teaspoon ground nutmeg

Preheat oven to 350°F

**1.** Dice French bread in cubes and place on the bottom of a 4-quart casserole dish.

**2.** Peel and grate apples and press in colander to drain.

**3.** Beat eggs, cream, almond extract, and seasonings until well mixed, about 2 minutes by hand. Pour over bread mixture.

**4.** Mix softened butter, apples, brown sugar, pecans, and spices. Spread over egg and bread mixture, tightly cover, and refrigerate overnight.

**5.** Bake at 350ºF for one hour or until brown and puffy. Serve with maple syrup if desired.

**To serve:** Serve with sliced Canadian bacon dusted with Cajun Sensation Spice Blend.

*Chef's secret: Save leftover French bread and freeze it until you have enough for a bake.*

### Shopping List

French bread loaf

large eggs

half-and-half cream

almond extract

ground cinnamon

ground nutmeg

salt

apples

butter

dark brown sugar

chopped pecans

# Mamou Crawfish Boudin Balls

Serves 8-10

Cajun music and spicy Boudin sausage go hand in hand at Fred's Lounge in Mamou, Louisiana, where every Saturday morning the Cajuns get together for a little music and a lot of dancing. When we visited there recently the local butcher shop sent some Boudin over to "taste" and to let us know we could stop by and pick some up and take it home after the show. Well, of course, the Boudin never made it that far.

Saltine crackers and creole mustard make this a great appetizer for brunch. To make things easy on the cook, this recipe is made as balls instead of links in casings.

## Ingredients

| | |
|---|---|
| 1 | pound crawfish tail meat (You can find this in the frozen fish section of your grocery store, all ready to go.) |
| 1 | large onion, diced |
| 3 | cups cooked rice |
| 2 | cups chicken stock |
| ½ | bunch parsley, chopped |
| 1 | bunch green onions, chopped |
| 2 | large eggs, beaten |
| 1 | tablespoon Cajun Sensation Spice Blend (page 10) |
| Oil for frying | |

**Stove top**

**1.** In a grinder or food processor, chop fine crawfish tail meat and onions.

**2.** Add rice and half of the chicken stock. Mix in the chopped parsley and chopped green onions.

**3.** Add beaten eggs and seasoning. Form balls about the size of a small meatball. Chill well.

**4.** In a medium sauté pan, add one tablespoon of oil and heat. Form crawfish mixture into balls and fry until brown. Makes approximately 30 balls, depending on the size rolled.

| Shopping List |
| --- |
| crawfish tail meat |
| large onion |
| green onions |
| fresh parsley |
| cooked rice |
| Cajun Sensation Spice Blend |
| chicken stock |
| large eggs |
| oil |

Note: If you can't find crawfish locally, see page 211 for mail-order information.

# Cheesy Garlic Grits and Grillades
# with Tomato Gravy

Serves 8-10

*Grillades are a mainstay of Southern brunches. Make this dish the day before and let the flavors "marry." My Aunt Edna made this for holiday brunches when the family used to get together after church and tell stories from days gone by. This dish is great for that brunch later in the day.*

## Ingredients

**Cheesy Garlic Grits**

| | |
|---|---|
| 6 | cups water |
| 4 | teaspoons coarse kosher salt |
| 2 | cups grits |
| 2 | cups milk |
| 4 | tablespoons butter |
| 1 | tablespoon minced garlic |
| 4 | large eggs |
| 2 | cups shredded cheddar cheese |

Preheat oven to 350°F

**1.** In a saucepan over medium high heat, bring water and salt to a boil. Slowly stir in grits.

**2.** Turn down heat to low, cover, and cook for approximately 5-7 minutes, stirring occasionally.

**3.** Remove from heat and allow to cool slightly.

**4.** Heat milk, butter, and garlic, add to warm grits, and stir until smooth.

**5.** Add eggs and cheese and mix. Spoon into a greased 2-quart casserole and bake at 350°F for approximately 1 hour until slightly browned.

# Grillades with Tomato Gravy

## Serves 4-6

Note—*recipe is easily doubled to match the portions of the Cheesy Garlic Grits.*

## Ingredients

| | |
|---|---|
| 2 pounds veal or beef round steak, cut into cubes | 1 tablespoon garlic, minced |
| 2 teaspoons kosher salt | 1 15-ounce can diced tomatoes in juice |
| 1 teaspoon black pepper | 2 tablespoons fresh basil |
| ½ cup bacon drippings or butter | 4 bay leaves |
| ½ cup flour | ½ tablespoon Cajun Sensation Spice Blend (page 10) |
| 1 cup onion, chopped | Tabasco and Worcestershire to taste |
| ½ cup celery, chopped | 1½ cups water |
| 1 cup total red, yellow, and green peppers, diced | ½ cup chopped parsley |
| 1 cup green onions, chopped | |

**Chef's secret:** *This dish has a much richer flavor the next day. To reheat, add a little chicken stock or water to grillades before heating.*

**To serve:** Serve with bakery or homemade biscuits for sopping up the delicious gravy!

Stove top

**1.** Season meat with salt and pepper. In large heavy pot, brown the meat in half of the drippings or butter. Remove and keep warm.

**2.** Add remaining drippings and flour to make a brown roux.

**3.** Add celery, peppers, chopped onions, and garlic; sauté until soft.

**4.** Add tomatoes and seasonings. Stir in water.

**5.** Place meat in roux and simmer for at least 1½ hours. Before serving, remove bay leaves and stir in parsley. Serve hot with grits.

## Shopping List
### Cheesy Garlic Grits and Grillades with Tomato Gravy

| | |
|---|---|
| kosher salt | onions |
| grits | celery |
| milk | red, yellow, green peppers |
| butter | green onions |
| large eggs | canned diced tomatoes in juice |
| garlic | fresh basil |
| shredded cheddar cheese | bay leaves |
| veal or beef round steak | Cajun Sensation Spice Blend |
| black pepper | Tabasco sauce |
| bacon drippings or butter | Worcestershire sauce |
| all-purpose flour | chopped parsley |

# Bananas Pontchartrain

Serves 8-10

Bananas and plantains grow well in the subtropical climate of Southern Louisiana. With their natural sweetness, bananas are stars at breakfast time, often paired up with grilled breakfast meats. On the weekends that I didn't work brunches, I was always at someone's house or restaurant for one. It was our way to relax and enjoy the day.

## Ingredients

| | |
|---|---|
| 8 | bananas, cut into thirds |
| 6 | tablespoons orange juice |
| 1 | tablespoon grated orange peel |
| 1 | teaspoon cinnamon |
| ½ | teaspoon nutmeg |
| ½ | cup brown sugar |
| 2 | cups crushed corn flakes |
| 4 | tablespoons butter, melted |

**Chef's secret:** *Crushing corn flakes is easier in a sealed plastic bag. Just roll over the bag with a rolling pin.*

Preheat oven to 350°F

**1.** Place bananas in 13 x 9" dish. Sprinkle with orange juice, orange peel, spices, and brown sugar.

**2.** Roll each banana piece in corn flakes and place back in dish. Melt butter and drizzle on bananas.

**3.** Bake at 350°F for 30 minutes until brown and puffy. Serve hot.

**To serve:** Serve with praline ice cream and butterscotch caramel sauce for dessert.

## Shopping List

bananas
orange juice
grated orange peel
ground cinnamon
ground nutmeg
brown sugar
crushed corn flakes
butter

# Eggs Cocodrie

Serves 6

*Poached egg dishes were made famous by the Brennan family. They served them in all of their restaurants, and they were delicious. These dishes have stood the test of time and are still on the menus of many restaurants in New Orleans. This is my version of one of those beautiful dishes I loved to eat.*

## Ingredients

| | |
|---|---|
| 12 | Holland rusks (a dry toast biscuit similar to an English muffin) |
| 2 | tablespoons butter |
| 1 | cup onion, chopped |
| 1 | cup celery, chopped |
| 1 | tablespoon garlic, chopped |
| 1 | green pepper, chopped |
| 4 | cups Cajun Cream Sauce (page 12) |
| 1 | 15-ounce can artichoke hearts |
| 1 | pound peeled and deveined shrimp, raw or cooked |
| 3 | tablespoons fresh herbs (basil, chives) |
| 1 | teaspoon Cajun Sensation Spice Blend (page 10) |
| 1 | teaspoon kosher salt |
| 2 | tablespoons fresh lemon juice |
| 12 | poached eggs |
| 6 | tablespoons shredded Parmesan cheese |

### Stove top

**1.** In a large saucepan, melt butter and sauté onion, celery, garlic, and pepper until soft.

**2.** Add Cajun Cream Sauce and heat thoroughly.

**3.** Slice artichoke hearts and add to sauce.

**4.** Add shrimp and cook until pink. Add spices, herbs, and lemon juice.

**5.** Spoon mixture over rusks, and top with poached eggs and shredded Parmesan cheese.

## Shopping List

| | |
|---|---|
| Holland rusks | peeled and deveined shrimp, raw or cooked |
| butter | fresh basil and chives |
| large onion | Cajun Sensation Spice Blend |
| celery | kosher salt |
| garlic | fresh lemon juice |
| green pepper | eggs |
| Cajun Cream Sauce | shredded Parmesan cheese |
| canned artichoke hearts | |

**To serve:** Serve with Bananas Pontchartrain (page 25).

*Chef's secret:* English muffins or large biscuits can be substituted for Holland rusks.

# Breakfast Cheesecake
# with Crawfish Piquant Sauce

### Serves 6

*S*avory *cheesecakes are coming into vogue in the restaurant scene. The sauce is a traditional piquant sauce, but it gets new life and rave reviews on this bed of silky, rich cheesecake.*

## Ingredients

**Crust**

| | |
|---|---|
| 1 | cup pecans |
| 1 | cup butter flavored crackers |
| 4 | tablespoons butter |

**Filling**

| | |
|---|---|
| 4 | ounces cream cheese, softened |
| ½ | cup sour cream |
| 3 | eggs |
| ½ | cup heavy cream |
| 1 | teaspoon kosher salt |
| 1 | teaspoon dry mustard |
| ½ | teaspoon white pepper |

Preheat oven to 350°F

**1.** In a food processor, process nuts and crackers separately until coarsely ground.

**2.** Melt butter and add to nuts and crackers. Stir and press into 9-inch pie pan.

**3.** Put cream cheese in a mixing bowl and mix until smooth. Add sour cream and blend well. Add eggs one at a time and blend. Add seasonings.

**4.** Pour slowly into prepared crust and bake in a preheated 350°F oven for 30-45 minutes or until cake sets. Let stand 15 minutes before cutting.

# Crawfish Piquant Sauce

## Ingredients

| | |
|---|---|
| 2 | tablespoons butter |
| 1 | medium onion, chopped |
| 3 | celery ribs, chopped |
| 1 | red pepper, chopped |
| 1 | tablespoon garlic, minced |
| 4 | tablespoons Dry Roux (page 7) |
| 1 | tablespoon Italian seasoning or dry oregano |
| 2 | teaspoons kosher salt |
| 1 | teaspoon Cajun Sensation Spice Blend (page 10) |
| 2 | tablespoons tomato paste |
| 2 | cups chicken stock or water |
| 1 | pound crawfish tail meat, cooked (thawed, if using frozen) |
| ½ | cup white wine |
| | Hot sauce to taste |

## Shopping List

| | |
|---|---|
| pecans | red pepper |
| butter flavored crackers | garlic |
| butter | Dry Roux |
| cream cheese | Italian seasoning or dry oregano |
| sour cream | kosher salt |
| large eggs | Cajun Sensation Spice Blend |
| heavy cream | tomato paste |
| kosher salt | chicken stock |
| dry mustard | crawfish tail meat |
| white pepper | white wine |
| medium onion | Louisiana hot sauce |
| celery | |

Stove top

**1.** In a large saucepan over medium heat, sauté vegetables in butter until soft.

**2.** Add dry roux and blend thoroughly.

**3.** Add spices, tomato paste, and chicken stock or water.

**4.** Cook for 20 minutes over low heat; add crawfish tail meat and white wine. Season to taste with hot sauce.

**To serve:** Spoon sauce over cheesecake wedges and serve with French 75s and Cheese Pennies (pages 200 and 44).

*Chef's secret: Crawfish tail meat can be purchased frozen in convenient one-pound packages.*

See page 211 for mail-order sources for Louisiana products.

# Red River Hash

Serves 4-6

The famous Red River runs through central Louisiana. It is in an area called the "Piney Woods" where there is lots of red clay in the dirt.

*I spent time every summer there with my cousins, exploring and having a terrific time, playing underneath the towering pine trees. My aunt used to make a dish very similar to this one for us for breakfast before a hard day of fun.*

## Ingredients

| | | | | |
|---|---|---|---|---|
| 2 | large sweet potatoes, peeled and diced | 1 | tablespoon garlic, chopped | |
| 1 | pound ham or Cajun smoked sausage links, diced in small pieces | 1 | green pepper, chopped | |
| | | 1 | cup whole kernel corn (fresh or frozen) | |
| ½ | cup onion, chopped | 2 | tablespoons dark corn syrup | |
| ½ | cup celery, chopped | 1 | teaspoon kosher salt | |

### Stove top

**1.** Boil sweet potatoes until tender, but still firm (about 10 minutes).

**2.** Fry diced ham or sausage over medium heat in a large skillet for about 5 minutes. Remove and keep warm.

**3.** In the same skillet, fry onion, celery, garlic, and pepper. Add corn.

**4.** Add potatoes and cooked sausage to mixture and stir until hot.

**5.** Add corn syrup and salt.

**To serve:** Serve with poached eggs and lots of hot sauce.

**Chef's secret:** *Do not stir potatoes too much as they will become mushy.*

### Shopping List

| | |
|---|---|
| sweet potatoes | green pepper |
| ham or smoked sausage links | whole kernel corn, fresh or frozen |
| onion | dark corn syrup |
| celery | kosher salt |
| garlic | |

# Caramelized Peaches and Cream

Yields 6-8 servings

*Peaches and cream are a natural combination. This unusual brunch dish is always a hit and showcases that fresh fruit flavor.*

## Ingredients

| | |
|---|---|
| 3 | cups fresh peaches, sliced |
| 1 | cup sour cream |
| 1 | teaspoon almond extract |
| ½ | teaspoon cinnamon |
| ½ | teaspoon ground ginger |
| 1 | cup light brown sugar, packed |

Heat oven broiler

**1.** Place sliced peaches in a pie pan or in an ovenproof baking dish.

**2.** Combine sour cream, almond extract, and spices. Pour over the fruit.

**3.** Sprinkle with brown sugar. Broil in oven until sugar melts, being careful not to burn.

**4.** Let cool and refrigerate for 4 hours before serving.

**To serve:** Serve with baked egg dishes and sausage.

*Chef's secret: Other fruits, such as apples or pears work as well for this dish.*

## Shopping List

fresh peaches
sour cream
almond extract
cinnamon
ginger
light brown sugar

# Savory Sausage Patties

Makes 1 pound

*T*asty sausages are a mainstay in Louisiana cooking. They allow the butchers to be resourceful *and creative at the same time. Spices add zip to this recipe that makes it "dance in your mouth." Be sure and get the meat ground fresh from your butcher.*

## Ingredients

| | |
|---|---|
| 1 | pound ground pork (about 20% fat or less) |
| 1 | teaspoon red pepper |
| ¼ | teaspoon mace |
| ½ | teaspoon crushed sage |
| ¼ | teaspoon ground ginger |
| ⅓ | teaspoon ground cardamom |
| ⅓ | teaspoon ground cinnamon |
| 1 | tablespoon dark corn syrup |
| ½ | teaspoon kosher salt |

Stove top

Mix all ingredients until blended. Form into patties and fry.

**To serve:** Serve with buttermilk biscuits.

*Chef's secret: Minced apple can be added for extra flavor.*

## Shopping List

ground pork (20% fat or less)
red pepper
mace
crushed sage
ground ginger
ground cardamom
ground cinnamon
dark corn syrup
kosher salt

# Appetizers and Party Food

Small dishes, grazing, and hors d'oeuvre parties have become a mainstay of contemporary entertaining. Holidays, special occasions, and ceremonies have beckoned the cooks of Louisiana for years, providing them opportunities to show off their great skills. I remember throwing my first dinner party when I was fourteen. It was for six of my friends, and I made all of the courses from scratch, including the dessert. I realized then that I perhaps had a talent for cooking. When we hosted larger events for graduations and weddings it was a production that often started a month ahead with the baking of sweets.

My favorite time to entertain is when out-of-town company comes to visit. We have a lot of international guests, so I like to give parties for all of our friends in their honor. Sometimes I make them teach me a new dish, or I put together easy appetizers that can be made in advance so I can enjoy the party also. To me, appetizers need to be fast and fabulous. Here are a few hints for survival as a busy entertainer today:

Come up with a strategy. Either you will cook or have part or all of it catered. (This could mean picking up trays from the local gourmet shop, or hiring staff to help with the dishes.) Be realistic about what you can handle without getting frazzled.

Plan your work and work your plan. In other words, make a list!

Keep a well-stocked cook's pantry. Sauces and frozen items can always come out at the last minute to add on when a few more guests show up.

Dress up the room with flowers and props. For a Louisiana theme party, Mardi Gras beads, doubloons, and masks make a great table. My friend Kay Biga decorates her table with different kinds of hot sauces on bright glass plates and uses fresh peppers to add a festive touch.

Do as much ahead of time as possible. Prepare only a few things (if any) during the party. Your guests want you to have fun too, even at your own party!

# Artichoke and Red Pepper Finger Pies

Makes 48 pieces

## Ingredients

| | | | |
|---|---|---|---|
| 1 | tablespoon vegetable oil | ⅛ | teaspoon cayenne pepper |
| 1 | cup onion, diced small | 1 | cup pepper jack cheese, shredded |
| 1 | rib celery, minced | | |
| ½ | roasted red pepper, minced | 2 | packages frozen puff pastry sheets |
| 1 | tablespoon chopped garlic | | |
| 1 | 15-ounce can artichoke hearts, drained and chopped | 2 | eggs, beaten with 2 tablespoons water |
| 1 | teaspoon kosher salt | | |

Preheat oven to 400°F

**1.** In skillet, sauté onion, celery, pepper, garlic, and artichoke hearts in vegetable oil over medium heat about 10 minutes.

**2.** Remove from heat and add seasonings.

**3.** Let cool, then add shredded cheese.

**4.** Thaw pastry as directed on box and roll out on a lightly floured surface one sheet at time. With a small biscuit cutter or glass, cut out a 3-inch circle. You should get about 12 circles from each sheet.

**5.** With a pastry brush, brush egg wash (egg beaten with water) on each circle and place 1 teaspoon of filling on each circle. Fold over and crimp with a fork or use a pastry press. Brush the top of the pastry with egg wash and place on an ungreased cookie sheet.

**6.** Place in a 400°F oven for 15 minutes until pies turn golden brown and puffy. Serve hot.

*Chef's secret:* To roast a red pepper, place under broiler for a few minutes, turning once or twice, until skin is blistered and dark. Place in a brown paper bag for fifteen minutes. The pepper will peel easily.

### Shopping List

| | |
|---|---|
| vegetable oil | kosher salt |
| onion | cayenne pepper |
| celery | pepper jack cheese |
| red pepper | frozen puff pastry sheets |
| garlic | eggs |
| canned artichoke hearts | |

# Smoked Crawfish Cakes with Lemon Herb Cream

Makes 12 appetizers or 24-30 mini cakes

## Ingredients

### Smoked Crawfish Cakes

2   tablespoons vegetable oil
3   tablespoons shallots, minced
½   cup green, yellow, and red pepper, minced
1   pound crawfish tail meat
2   large zucchini, shredded and drained
¼   cup heavy cream
1   cup bread crumbs
3   eggs
1   tablespoon Cajun Sensation Spice blend (page 10)
Dash of hot sauce and Worcestershire sauce
2   teaspoons kosher salt

½   cup shredded Parmesan cheese
1   teaspoon liquid smoke
Oil for frying

### Lemon Herb Cream

2   cups heavy cream
½   cup shredded Parmesan cheese
1   teaspoon garlic, minced
½   bunch green onions, sliced
Kosher salt and red pepper to taste
2   tablespoons fresh lemon zest
2   tablespoons fresh dill
1   bunch fresh watercress, chopped

Stove top

**1.** In a large skillet over medium heat, fry shallots and peppers in vegetable oil until soft.

**2.** Add crawfish tails and cook about 5 minutes. Remove and transfer to a large bowl. Add shredded zucchini, cream, bread crumbs, and eggs. Add seasonings and Parmesan cheese.

**3.** Heat oil in a skillet over medium heat, covering the bottom, and drop mixture by the tablespoon into the hot oil, frying on one side and turning over and frying on the other side until golden brown.

**Lemon Herb Cream:**

**1.** In a small saucepan, heat cream for 30 minutes, reducing to half. Add Parmesan cheese, garlic, green onion, and seasonings.

**2.** Stir in lemon zest and dill.

**3.** Drizzle on cakes and garnish with chopped watercress.

### Shopping List

| | |
|---|---|
| vegetable oil | Louisiana hot sauce |
| shallots | Worcestershire sauce |
| green, yellow, and red peppers | shredded Parmesan cheese |
| crawfish tail meat* | liquid smoke |
| zucchini | vegetable oil for frying |
| heavy cream | garlic |
| bread crumbs | green onions |
| eggs | kosher salt and red pepper |
| Cajun Sensation Spice Blend | fresh dill |
| | fresh watercress |

\* See page 211 for mail order sources.

# Crab Beignets
# with Scallion and Garlic Mayonnaise

### Makes 8-10 appetizer portions

*This is a savory cousin of the sweet doughnut served at famous New Orleans restaurants. It's a garlic lover's favorite. By the way, did you know that Louisiana is one of the largest producers of garlic in the U.S.? Garlic is a member of the lily family, and there are three types of garlic available in the U.S. They are American, Italian, and Mexican.*

## Ingredients

**Crab Beignets**

1 cup flour
1 teaspoon baking powder
½ teaspoon kosher salt
1 teaspoon vegetable oil
¼ cup milk
2 large eggs
4 ounces crabmeat
¾ cup grated cheddar cheese
¼ diced red pepper
1 tablespoon garlic, crushed
¼ teaspoon black pepper
¼ teaspoon cayenne pepper
Pinch of each—thyme, oregano, basil, chervil

Oil for frying

**Scallion Garlic Mayonnaise**

½ cup mayonnaise
1 tablespoon creole or brown mustard
3 green onions, sliced thin
1 tablespoon crushed garlic
¼ teaspoon kosher salt
Dash of hot sauce and Worcestershire
1 teaspoon lime juice
1 teaspoon lime zest

Pickapeppa sauce

**Stove top**

**1.** In a large bowl, add all ingredients in order and blend.

**2.** Drop by large tablespoons into 400°F oil, frying until golden brown; turn once.

**3.** Drain on paper towels; serve hot.

**Scallion Garlic Mayonnaise:**

Blend all ingredients together in bowl. Serve with beignets along with the Pickapeppa sauce.

**Chef's secret:** *Substitute crawfish tail meat for crab or use a mixture of crab and shrimp.*

### Shopping List

| | |
|---|---|
| all-purpose flour | cayenne pepper |
| baking powder | thyme, oregano, basil, chervil |
| kosher salt | oil for frying |
| vegetable oil | mayonnaise |
| milk | creole or brown mustard |
| large eggs | green onions |
| crabmeat | Louisiana hot sauce |
| grated cheddar cheese | Worcestershire sauce |
| red pepper | lime juice |
| garlic | lime zest |
| black pepper | Pickapeppa sauce |

# Cheese Truffles with Chicken and Pecans

Makes 24 balls

## Ingredients

| | |
|---|---|
| 1 | cup cooked ground chicken |
| 8 | ounces soft cheese such as cream, Cherve, or blended mix of each |
| ½ | teaspoon curry powder |
| 3 | tablespoons hot pepper jelly |
| ½ | cup sliced green onions |
| 1 | teaspoon creole or brown mustard |
| 1 | teaspoon kosher salt |
| 1 | cup roasted pecans, finely chopped |

Parsley for garnish

Directions for roasting nuts on page 194.

No cooking

**1.** Mix chicken, cheese, curry powder, hot pepper jelly, green onions, mustard, and salt.

**2.** Chill. Scoop with spoon and roll in pecans. Garnish with chopped parsley.

**Chef's secret:** *These can be made in advance and stored in the refrigerator for a day or so or in the freezer for up to a month. Cilantro can also be added for a zesty flavor.*

## Shopping List

cooked chicken, ground

cream or Cherve cheese

curry powder

hot pepper jelly

green onions

creole or brown mustard

kosher salt

pecan pieces

chopped parsley

# Eggplant Chips

Serves 4-6

*Eggplant is abundant in Louisiana at harvest time. In fact, when you go to church you had better lock your car doors, or when you return you may find a basket of them on your back seat!*

## Ingredients

1   large eggplant
2   teaspoons kosher salt
2   large eggs
½   cup half-and-half cream
½   teaspoon hot sauce
1   teaspoon Cajun Sensation Spice Blend (page 10)
½   teaspoon ground cumin
1   cup of seasoned bread crumbs
Splash of cider vinegar
Oil for frying

## Stove top

**1.** Peel eggplant and slice in half. Slice each half into 4 slabs. Cut into sticks about ½ inch thick.

**2.** Place on paper towels and sprinkle with salt. Let stand 20 minutes and turn; pat dry. This will take any bitterness out.

**3.** Mix in a large bowl eggs, cream, hot sauce, spice mix, and cumin.

**4.** Dip each eggplant stick into the egg mixture and then in the seasoned bread crumbs.

**5.** Deep fry in 400ºF oil until golden brown. Remove and drain on paper towels. Splash with cider vinegar before serving.

## Shopping List

eggplant
kosher salt
large eggs
half-and-half cream
Louisiana hot sauce
Cajun Sensation Spice Blend
ground cumin
seasoned bread crumbs
cider vinegar
oil

# Cheese Pennies

Yields 7 dozen

*Cheese Pennies are a very tasty addition to Bloody Marys for brunch. In New Orleans, they are often served at cocktail receptions and given at holiday time for hostess gifts.*

## Ingredients

| | |
|---|---|
| ½ | pound shredded sharp cheddar cheese |
| ½ | cup butter, softened |
| ¼ | cup sesame seeds, toasted |
| 1¼ | cups flour |
| 1 | teaspoon kosher salt |
| ½ | teaspoon garlic powder |
| ½ | teaspoon cayenne pepper |

Preheat oven to 350°F

**1.** Bring shredded cheese to room temperature. Combine with butter, sesame seeds, flour, salt, and spices.

**2.** Mix dough with mixer until blended well; it will change colors after about 4 minutes and turn into a soft dough.

**3.** Form dough into 3 rolls and wrap in plastic wrap.

**4.** Chill for one hour.

**5.** Cut into ¼-inch slices and place on a cookie sheet. Bake at 350°F for 12 to 15 minutes until golden brown. Store in an airtight container.

## Shopping List

shredded sharp cheddar cheese
butter
sesame seeds
all-purpose flour
kosher salt
garlic powder
cayenne pepper

**Chef's secret:** *To toast sesame seeds spread on a foil-covered baking sheet and toast in oven at 350°F for a few minutes. Watch carefully as they burn easily.*

# Sweet and Sour Red Peppers

Makes 8-10 appetizer servings

This is a do-ahead appetizer that is popular in the fall when the red peppers are at their best.

### Ingredients

| | |
|---|---|
| 4 | red peppers, chopped fine |
| ¾ | cup white sugar |
| ½ | cup vinegar (white wine or rice) |
| ½ | teaspoon seasoned salt |
| 8 | ounces cream cheese |
| 1 | ounce Pickapeppa sauce |
| 1 | box Triscuit crackers |

Stove top

**1.** Simmer peppers, sugar, vinegar, and salt for about 50 minutes until thick. Let cool.

**2.** Pour over block of cream cheese and splash on Pickapeppa just before serving. Serve with crackers.

**To serve:** Serve with chopped parsley as garnish for a festive holiday touch.

*Chef's secret: Red pepper sauce can be frozen.*

### Shopping List

red peppers
sugar
vinegar (white wine or rice)
seasoned salt
cream cheese
Pickapeppa sauce
Triscuit crackers

# Louisiana Egg Rolls
# with Pineapple Dipping Sauce

Serves 12

*This is a twist on an Asian classic. Egg rolls have become a mainstay of trendy restaurant menus. They are surprisingly easy to make.*

## Ingredients

| | |
|---|---|
| 1 | package egg roll skins |
| 2 | tablespoons vegetable oil |
| ½ | cup grated onion, drained |
| ½ | cup roasted red pepper, minced |
| 1 | tablespoon minced garlic |
| 5 | cups shredded green cabbage |
| ½ | cup red beans, cooked, drained, and mashed (canned are OK) |

| | |
|---|---|
| 6 | ounces cooked shrimp, chopped |
| 1 | teaspoon Cajun Sensation Spice Blend (page 10) |
| 1 | teaspoon creole or brown mustard |
| 1 | egg beaten with 1 tablespoon water |
| | Oil for deep-frying |

**To serve:** Serve with creole or brown mustard and Pineapple Dipping Sauce (recipe follows).

*Chef's secret: Crawfish can be substituted for shrimp.*

### Stove top

**1.** In a large skillet, sauté onion, red pepper, and garlic in oil until soft. Place in a large mixing bowl.

**2.** Blanch cabbage in boiling water for 2 minutes; drain and add to vegetable mixture.

**3.** Add mashed red beans, shrimp, spice blend, and mustard to mix.

**4.** Place about two tablespoons of vegetable mix on lower part of wrapper. Folding sides, roll up and seal with egg wash.

**5.** Deep fry in 400ºF oil about 2 minutes on each side. Drain on paper towels.

# Pineapple Dipping Sauce

## Ingredients

1   6-ounce can crushed pineapple with juice
1   tablespoon brown sugar
1   tablespoon ketchup
2   tablespoons white vinegar
2   teaspoons cornstarch

Stove top

1. Mix all ingredients in a small saucepan and heat to a boil.

2. Let cool and serve.

*Chef's secret:* For extra zip, serve with bottled Pickapeppa sauce.

## Shopping List

packaged egg roll skins
vegetable oil
white onions
roasted red peppers
garlic
green cabbage
red beans
cooked shrimp
Cajun Sensation Spice Blend

creole or brown mustard
egg
oil for deep frying
canned crushed pineapple with juice
brown sugar
ketchup
white vinegar
cornstarch

# Caviar Pie Dip

Yields approximately 10 servings

My friend Ann Willett inspired me in the development of this spectacular appetizer. It is certainly elegant and simple.

### Ingredients

½ ounce each of red, black, and gold lump fish caviar
1 pint sour cream
1 cup bacon, cooked well and chopped
½ bunch green onions, sliced thin
2 eggs, boiled, chopped fine
Sliced lemons for garnish

Stove top

1. Gently rinse caviars well in a small sieve. Set aside.

2. Mix sour cream, bacon, green onions, and eggs to make a dip.

3. Spread in a shallow dish and top with drained caviar just before serving.

**To serve:** Serve with water crackers.

*Chef's secret:* A small block of softened cream cheese could be added for a heavier dip.

### Shopping List

black, gold, and red lump fish caviar
bacon
sour cream
green onions
eggs
lemons

# Carol's Parmesan Cheese Spread

Yields approximately 2 cups

*My good friend Carol Harris gave me this recipe. It's healthy and tasty. Be sure to use the real grated Parmesan; it makes a difference in the taste.*

## Ingredients

| | |
|---|---|
| 12 | ounces fat-free cream cheese, softened |
| 1 | cup grated Parmesan cheese |
| ¼ | cup low fat mayonnaise |
| ½ | teaspoon oregano, crumbled |
| ⅛ | teaspoon garlic powder |
| ½ | cup sliced or whole toasted almonds |

Directions for toasting nuts on page 194.

No cook

**1.** In a medium bowl, blend cream cheese, Parmesan cheese, mayonnaise, oregano, and garlic powder.

**2.** Top with sliced or whole toasted almonds. Chill for 1 hour or longer.

**To serve:** Serve with fresh vegetables or crackers.

**Chef's secret:** *This spread can be made a day ahead.*

## Shopping List

fat-free cream cheese
Parmesan cheese
low-fat mayonnaise
oregano
garlic powder
sliced or whole almonds

# Hot and Sweet Spiced Pecans

Yields 8 cups

*One of my chores in my younger years was to assist in pecan harvesting. We would spend hours picking up pecans that had fallen from the towering old trees. Afterwards we would crack and shell the nuts, carefully labeling and freezing for delicious dishes to come. This recipe makes a terrific holiday gift from the kitchen.*

## Ingredients

| | |
|---|---|
| 2 | pounds pecan halves and pieces |
| 4 | tablespoons butter, melted |
| 1 | teaspoon cayenne pepper |
| 1 | tablespoon garlic salt |
| 2 | tablespoons brown sugar |

Heat oven to 350°F

**1.** Melt butter and pour over pecans.

**2.** Sprinkle with pepper, garlic salt, and brown sugar. Spread on a foil-covered baking sheet. Bake 30 minutes, turning often to evenly coat the nuts. Store in an airtight container.

**To serve:** Serve with cocktails at holiday time.

**Chef's secret:** *Olive oil can also be used.*

## Shopping List

pecan halves and pieces
butter
cayenne pepper
garlic salt
brown sugar

# Hot Onion Puffs

Yields 2 dozen

*This appetizer is a mainstay in our house. It is quick and you usually have the ingredients on hand to prepare it.*

## Ingredients

| | |
|---|---|
| 1 | large Vidalia or other sweet onion, finely chopped |
| ¼ | cup low-fat mayonnaise |
| 1 | large egg yolk |
| ½ | teaspoon sugar |
| 1 | teaspoon Cajun Sensation Spice Blend (page 10) |
| 24 | slices party rye or sourdough bread |
| ⅓ | cup grated Parmesan cheese |

Heat oven to 375°F

**1.** Mix onion, mayonnaise, egg yolk, sugar, and spice blend in a mixing bowl.

**2.** Top bread slices with onion mixture and sprinkle with Parmesan cheese.

**3.** Bake on cookie sheet in oven 15-20 minutes until puffy.

**To serve:** Serve with crispy carrot sticks and dip.

*Chef's secret: Other spices can be substituted.*

## Shopping List

Vidalia or other sweet onion
low-fat mayonnaise
egg
sugar
Cajun Sensation Spice Blend
party rye or sourdough bread
Parmesan cheese

# Spicy Stuffed Mushrooms

Yields 1 dozen

## Ingredients

| | | | | |
|---|---|---|---|---|
| 1 | pound smoked Cajun sausage or other smoked sausage, diced small | 1 | pound mushrooms, diced | |
| 2 | tablespoons (¼ stick) butter | 1 | pound shrimp, medium size, peeled and deveined | |
| 1 | medium red bell pepper, diced small | ½ | cup water | |
| 1 | green bell pepper, diced small | 1 | cup bread crumbs | |
| 1 | jalapeño pepper, minced | 1 | cup grated Jack and Parmesan cheese, mixed | |
| 1 | bunch green onions, sliced | | Salt and pepper | |
| 1 | tablespoon garlic, minced | 1 | dozen fresh Portobello mushrooms | |

Preheat oven to 450°F

**1.** Sauté sausage until cooked; remove and reserve.

**2.** Heat butter; add vegetables and cook until soft.

**3.** Add shrimp, water, and sausage; cook until water has evaporated.

**4.** Remove from heat and add cheese and bread crumbs. You may need to add more cheese and bread crumbs for it to be firm enough to stick together. Season with salt and pepper.

**5.** Mound stuffing (about 2 or 3 ounces) on stem side of mushrooms. Place on a cookie sheet and bake in a 450°F oven for about 15 minutes or until the stuffing is brown and bubbly.

**6.** Cool slightly and cut in wedges to serve.

**To serve:** Serve with celery sticks and a tasty cheese dip.

*Chef's secret: Cracker crumbs can be substituted for bread crumbs.*

### Shopping List

| | |
|---|---|
| smoked Cajun sausage | mushrooms |
| butter | shrimp, medium sized |
| red bell pepper | bread crumbs |
| green bell pepper | grated Jack cheese |
| jalapeño pepper | grated Parmesan cheese |
| green onions | Portobello mushrooms |
| garlic | |

# Shrimp with Fresh Herbs and Pernod

Yields 60 pieces

*This is very popular for formal cocktail parties. It makes a large batch, perfect for your next holiday soiree.*

## Ingredients

| | |
|---|---|
| 5 | pounds jumbo (#12) shrimp, peeled and deveined |
| 8 | ounces of the following fresh herbs, mixed: |
| | basil, cilantro, parsley, chives, rosemary |
| 1 | pound (4 sticks) unsalted butter |
| 5 | cloves garlic, minced |
| 8 | ounces Pernod (1 cup) |
| ½ | cup flour |
| Salt and white pepper to taste | |

Stove top

1. Chop herbs.

2. Heat butter in a large Dutch oven or roaster; add herbs and garlic.

3. Add shrimp and cook until pink.

4. Add Pernod. Sprinkle with flour and cook until thick. Season with salt and white pepper.

**To serve:** Serve with toothpicks for a stand-up cocktail party. Watch them go quickly!

## Shopping List

jumbo shrimp

fresh basil, parsley, rosemary, cilantro, chives

unsalted butter

garlic cloves

Pernod liquor

flour

white pepper

***Chef's secret:*** *The number designation for shrimp usually means how many per pound.*

# Party Time Crabby Dip

Yields approximately 1 quart

*H*ot *dips are popular during the holiday season. This one is quick and easy. It holds well in a crock pot, too.*

## Ingredients

| | |
|---|---|
| 3 | tablespoons butter |
| 2 | medium onions, minced |
| 1 | green pepper, minced |
| 4 | ribs celery, minced |
| 1 | pound crabmeat, picked and cleaned |
| 3 | 10-ounce cans cream of mushroom soup |
| ½ | cup shredded Parmesan cheese |

Worcestershire sauce to taste

Hot sauce to taste

Salt and white pepper

| | |
|---|---|
| ½ | bunch fresh parsley, chopped |
| 1 | cup shredded Swiss cheese |
| 1 | cup milk |

### Stove top

**1.** Melt butter in a large saucepan, add vegetables, and cook until soft.

**2.** Add crabmeat, soup, and Parmesan cheese; heat gently. Add seasonings.

**3.** When warmed, transfer to crock pot, and just before serving stir in fresh parsley, Swiss cheese, and milk to desired thickness.

**To serve:** Serve with buttery crackers.

**Chef's secret:** *Imitation crab can be substituted with good results.*

## Shopping List

butter

medium sized onions

green pepper

celery

crabmeat

cream of mushroom soup

Parmesan cheese

Worcestershire sauce

hot sauce

salt

white pepper

fresh parsley

Swiss cheese

milk

# Eggplant Dumaine

Yields 3-4 cups

*E*very culture has its own eggplant dip. The Cajun version has all of the local vegetables plus a few more spices. This dish is Italian influenced.

## Ingredients

| | |
|---|---|
| 1½ | pounds eggplant (2-3) |
| 3 | tablespoons olive oil, divided |
| 1 | tablespoon garlic, minced |
| 4 | plum tomatoes, quartered |
| 2 | ribs celery, minced |
| 1 | medium onion, chopped fine |
| 1 | green pepper, chopped fine |
| 1 | teaspoon Cajun Sensation Spice Blend (page 10) |
| 3 | tablespoons fresh basil, chopped |
| ¼ | cup sliced black olives |
| 2 | tablespoons balsamic vinegar |
| 1 | teaspoon sugar |

**To serve:** Serve with sliced French bread or pita bread.

Preheat oven to 450°F

**1.** Cut eggplants in half, prick, and spray with a nonstick spray. Roast cut side down on a baking sheet until tender (30-40 minutes). Set aside to cool slightly.

**2.** In a large skillet, sauté garlic, tomatoes, celery, onion, and green pepper in 1 tablespoon of olive oil until soft.

**3.** Add spice blend, fresh basil, olives, balsamic vinegar, sugar, and remaining 2 tablespoons of olive oil.

**4.** Remove baked eggplant from skin, mash, and blend into above mixture.

## Shopping List

eggplants
olive oil
garlic
plum tomatoes
celery
onion
green pepper
Cajun Sensation Spice Blend
fresh basil
sliced black olives
balsamic vinegar
sugar

***Chef's secret:*** *This dip will keep for several days; just season before serving.*

# Summertime Shrimp Mousse

Yields 10 servings

*F*resh shrimp really makes this dish special. We served it in New Orleans for lunch with crispy fresh vegetables and sliced French bread.

## Ingredients

| | |
|---|---|
| 1 | pound raw shrimp in shells (any size) |
| 16 | ounces cream cheese, softened |
| ½ | cup sour cream |
| 1 | 12-ounce bottle chili sauce |
| 1 | green pepper, chopped fine |
| 3 | ribs celery, chopped fine |
| 1 | bunch green onions, sliced thin |
| 3 | tablespoons unflavored gelatin |
| 1 | cup shrimp stock |

**Chef's secret:** *Spicy chili sauce will give this dish some heat.*

### Stove top

**1.** Cook shrimp, reserving 1 cup of stock. Shell and chop shrimp fine.

**2.** Mix cream cheese, sour cream, and chili sauce. Add chopped vegetables and shrimp.

**3.** Mix shrimp stock and gelatin together; bring to a boil, then turn heat off and let cool slightly.

**4.** Combine stock mixture with vegetable cheese mix and pour into 2 plastic wrap-lined loaf pans (1 pound size).

**5.** Let chill for 3 hours.

**To serve:** Serve a slice of the loaf on a plate garnished with fresh herbs.

## Shopping List

raw shrimp in shells
cream cheese
sour cream
chili sauce
green pepper
celery
green onions
unflavored gelatin

**Chef's secret:** *To cook shirmp, place in a pot of boiling water. When the water returns to a boil, remove from heat, cover, and let stand for 1 hour. Shrimp will always be tender cooked this way.*

# Sausage Balls of Fire

Yields approximately 50 balls

These tasty treats go great with cocktails or for a brunch appetizer.

## Ingredients

2½ cups baking mix
1 cup cheddar cheese, grated
1 pound bulk sausage
¼ teaspoon or more cayenne pepper
4 tablespoons fresh parsley, chopped

Preheat oven to 400°F

**1.** Mix all ingredients together. Roll into 1-inch balls.

**2.** Bake for 15 minutes or until brown at 400°F.

**To serve:** Serve with Bloody Marys.

**Chef's secret:** These may be frozen ahead before baking. Just add a few minutes to the cooking time.

## Shopping List

baking mix
cheddar cheese
bulk sausage
cayenne pepper
fresh parsley

# Soups, Stews, and One-Pot Meals

In Louisiana, there are countless recipes for gumbo. Many (and often very heated) discussions have been held to determine who has the tastiest version of this mainstay of Cajun and Creole cuisine.

I start my gumbo ritual when the first winter wind starts to chill the air. The menu is always the same—gumbo, baked sweet potatoes, and fresh hot French bread. With this meal, I am ready to settle in for the winter. It sets the tone for holiday cooking, which has become the entertaining season in our household. The word "gumbo" is a corruption of the African word "gombo" which means okra, a main ingredient. It has always been popular in the Cajun culture, especially during Lent when most people do not eat meat. It is truly an American dish made with an international blend of ingredients from several cuisines.

The following is a description of the common denominators of gumbo:

**The roux:** It is always made of equal parts of flour and oil (or butter). You can make it ahead of time in large quantities or as needed. It keeps well in and out of the refrigerator. If made in advance, always use hot water to dissolve.

**The body:** Gumbo can be made with chicken, duck, goose, crawfish, shrimp, oysters, ham, tasso (which is a spicy ham, available by mail order), sausage, or any wild game. Beef does not lend itself to good gumbo. You can also mix chicken and seafood stock for extra flavor.

**Thickening:** Gumbo is thickened with either okra or filé (it rhymes with relay). If using okra, fry it first or you will have "slimebo" instead of gumbo. Add it at the end of cooking. If using filé, sprinkle on individual bowls right before eating.

**Serving:** Place a generous helping of rice (Cajun caviar) in a bowl and ladle the gumbo over the rice. Don't remove the bay leaf, for while it is not eaten, it is a sign of good luck to whoever gets it. Serve with hot French bread and a green salad, and if you want to be a real Cajun, add a baked sweet potato on the side.

# Louisiana Gumbo

## The State Soup That Cooks with Jazz!

Yields 8 servings

### Ingredients

1¼ pounds fresh chicken, diced
1 cup butter or oil
1 cup flour
2 large chopped onions
6 ribs chopped celery
2 large chopped green peppers
1 tablespoon minced garlic
Seasonings: thyme, oregano, basil, bay leaves, red pepper, and kosher salt to taste

2 quarts chicken stock
1 pound smoked turkey sausage, sliced
1 pound sliced okra (frozen is OK)
3 cups cooked rice
Filé powder
Tabasco sauce

Stove top

**1.** Sauté chicken pieces in ½ cup of butter or oil until brown.

**2.** Add remainder of butter or oil and flour and make a medium brown roux, stirring constantly, approximately 20 minutes.

**3.** Add celery, onions, peppers, garlic, and seasonings. Cook until glazed. Slowly add chicken stock and sliced turkey sausage.

**4.** Sauté okra in a separate pan; add to gumbo and cook for one hour.

**To serve:** Serve over hot rice with a dash of filé powder on top and a splash of Tabasco.

*Chef's secret: Make your gumbo a day ahead of time, chill, and skim off the fat on top.*

### Shopping List

| | |
|---|---|
| chicken | bay leaves |
| butter or oil | red pepper |
| all-purpose flour | chicken stock |
| onions | smoked turkey sausage |
| celery | okra, fresh or frozen |
| green peppers | kosher salt |
| garlic | rice |
| thyme | filé powder |
| oregano | Tabasco sauce |
| basil | |

# Classic Crawfish Etouffée

Yields 6 servings

*Do you know what it means to miss New Orleans? To me it is this dish.*

## Ingredients

| | | |
|---|---|---|
| ½ | cup flour | |
| ½ | cup oil or butter | |
| 1 | yellow onion, chopped | |
| 1 | green pepper, chopped | |
| 2 | ribs celery, chopped | |
| 3 | cloves garlic, minced | |
| 1 | bunch green onions, sliced; separate the green and the white parts | |

| | |
|---|---|
| 2 | tablespoons tomato paste |
| 2 | cups chicken broth |
| 1 | pound crawfish tail meat, cooked |
| 1 | tablespoon Worcestershire |
| Hot sauce to taste | |
| ¼ | cup fresh chopped parsley |
| 4-6 | cups of rice, cooked |

Stove top

**1.** First, you have to make a roux. Mix butter or oil and flour together in a large cast iron skillet; cook over low heat for at least 20 minutes, stirring constantly.

**2.** After the roux is cooked, add the yellow onion, green pepper, celer, garlic, and white part of green onions; cook 10 minutes longer.

**3.** Add the tomato paste and chicken broth; simmer for 30 minutes.

**4.** About 5 minutes before serving, add crawfish tail meat, green onion tops, Worcestershire sauce and hot sauce, and chopped parsley.

**5.** Serve over hot rice.

**To serve:** Serve with a crusty, hot French bread.

**Chef's secret:** *Crawfish Etouffée is just as good or perhaps better served the next day. It also freezes quite well.*

## Shopping List

| | |
|---|---|
| all-purpose flour | tomato paste |
| oil or butter | chicken broth |
| yellow onion | crawfish tail meat |
| green pepper | Worcestershire sauce |
| celery | Louisiana hot sauce |
| garlic | fresh parsley |
| green onions | rice |

Note: If you cannot find fresh or frozen crawfish tail meat locally, see page 211 for seafood sources in Louisiana.

# Chicken and Artichoke Stew

Yields 4 servings

*Some Cajuns call a cross between a stew and an etouffée a "stoufée."*

*Dishes such as these were made on Sunday, when Mama had more time to cook and wanted to make something special.*

## Ingredients

| | | | | |
|---|---|---|---|---|
| 4 | 5-ounce boneless chicken breasts, sliced | | 1 | 28-ounce can diced tomatoes in juice |
| ½ | cup seasoned flour (1 teaspoon Cajun Sensation Spice Blend added) | | 2 | tablespoons fresh rosemary |
| | | | 1 | tablespoon capers |
| 4 | tablespoons butter | | 1 | teaspoon kosher salt |
| 1 | cup onion, chopped | | ½ | teaspoon ground black pepper |
| ½ | cup celery, chopped | | | |
| ½ | cup red or green pepper, chopped | | ½ | cup vermouth or dry white wine |
| 1 | tablespoon garlic, chopped | | 1 | pound bow tie pasta or 6 cups cooked rice |
| 1 | 15-ounce can artichoke hearts, sliced | | | |

Stove top

**1.** Dredge chicken in seasoned flour. Melt butter in skillet and sauté until browned.

**2.** Remove chicken and keep warm. Add onion, celery, pepper, and garlic and sauté until soft.

**3.** Add sliced artichoke hearts and the next 6 ingredients and simmer 30 minutes.

**4.** Serve over hot rice or pasta.

**To serve:** Serve with a Caesar salad and crusty French bread for a complete meal.

*Chef's secret:* Rice can be made up ahead of time and frozen in small plastic bags after cooking. Be sure to date the bags.

## Shopping List

butter
boneless chicken breasts
all-purpose flour
Cajun Sensation Spice Blend
onion
celery
red or green pepper
garlic

canned artichoke hearts
canned diced tomatoes in juice
fresh rosemary
capers
kosher salt
ground black pepper
vermouth or dry white wine
bow tie pasta or rice

# Redfish Courtboullion for a Crowd

Yields 12 servings

*This recipe hails from Dante By The River, a small barge board cottage restaurant that I used to work at many years ago in New Orleans. Redfish was the specialty of the house, so many dishes were invented using it. You may substitute catfish if redfish is not available in your area.*

## Ingredients

| | |
|---|---|
| ⅓ cup vegetable oil | 1 tablespoon dried marjoram |
| ½ cup flour | 4 whole bay leaves |
| 2 cups onion, chopped | 10 whole allspice |
| 1½ cups green onion tops | 3 tablespoons kosher salt |
| 1¾ cups green pepper, chopped | 3 tablespoons dried basil |
| 1 clove garlic, minced | ½ cup fresh lemon juice |
| 1½ cups celery, chopped | 1 28-ounce can peeled whole tomatoes, coarsely chopped |
| 2 tablespoons minced parsley (fresh) | 1½ cups dry red wine |
| 1 tablespoon dried thyme | 1 cup water |
| | 12 firm fish fillets (4-6 ounces each) |

Stove top

**1.** Heat the oil in a heavy 4-5-quart pot. Add the flour, stir, lower heat, and cook over a low heat until the roux is the color of peanut butter. (This will take about 25 minutes.)

**2.** Add the onion, green onion, green pepper, garlic, and celery and cook for 8-10 minutes.

**3.** Tie bay leaves and allspice in a piece of cheesecloth. Add the herbs, spices, tomatoes, lemon juice, and wine. Stir to mix and slowly add water, mixing well.

**4.** Bring to a boil, then lower heat and simmer uncovered for about 35 minutes. Stir often.

You can stop at this point and refrigerate the sauce until ready to cook the fish.

**5.** If chilled, reheat the sauce to simmer and poach the fish fillets in sauce for about 5 minutes, or until fish starts to flake.

**To serve:** Serve over a mound of steamed rice and garnish with fresh watercress.

*Chef's secret: Leftover sauce can be frozen with great success.*

## Shopping List

| | |
|---|---|
| vegetable oil | whole bay leaves |
| all-purpose flour | dried thyme |
| onion | dried marjoram |
| green onions | whole allspice |
| green pepper | kosher salt |
| garlic | dried basil |
| celery | fresh lemon juice |
| canned whole tomatoes | dry red wine |
| fresh parsley | fish fillets |

# Corn and Shrimp Chowder

Serves 12

This dish is borrowed from Louisiana's neighboring state, Texas. Shrimp is abundant in Southern Texas, with as many ways to prepare it.

## Ingredients

| | | | |
|---|---|---|---|
| 4 | tablespoons butter | 2 | cups water |
| 1 | cup onion, chopped | 1 | 15-ounce can creamed corn |
| ½ | cup green pepper, chopped | 1 | pound (about 7) red new potatoes |
| ½ | cup celery, chopped | 1 | pound medium shrimp, cleaned and deveined |
| ½ | cup red or yellow bell pepper, chopped | 2 | teaspoons kosher salt |
| 1 | tablespoon garlic, chopped | 1 | teaspoon Cajun Sass Seasoning Blend (page 11) |
| 1 | 15-ounce can or 1-pound package frozen whole kernel corn | 3 | tablespoons fresh parsley, chopped |
| 4 | tablespoons flour | 1 | bunch green onions, sliced |
| 2 | 14-ounce cans chicken broth | | |
| 1 | cup heavy cream | | |

Stove top

**1.** In large Dutch oven, melt butter and sauté onions, green and red pepper, celery, and garlic over medium heat until tender. Add whole kernel corn and cook, stirring well.

**2.** Add flour and stir until well blended.

**3.** Add chicken broth, heavy cream, water, and creamed corn, and mix well.

**4.** Peel and dice potatoes to a small size, about ½-inch cubes, and add to soup.

**5.** Turn heat to simmer and cook until potatoes are tender, about 45 minutes.

**6.** Add shrimp and seasonings and cook for 5 minutes. Add parsley and green onions right before serving.

**To serve:** Serve with crusty Italian bread and a Caesar salad.

*Chef's secret: If you purchase shrimp with their shells, you can make your own shrimp stock. Just boil shells with just enough water to cover for 30 minutes. Add salt and white pepper before using. Crabmeat can be substituted for shrimp.*

### Shopping List

| | |
|---|---|
| butter | heavy cream |
| onion | canned creamed corn |
| green pepper | red new potatoes |
| celery | medium shrimp, cleaned and deveined |
| red or yellow pepper | |
| garlic | kosher salt |
| canned or frozen whole kernel corn | Cajun Sass Seasoning Blend |
| all-purpose flour | fresh parsley |
| chicken broth | green onions |

# Shrimp and Oyster Creole Gumbo

Serves 8

*There are entire cookbooks devoted to the subject of gumbo. This is a tasty and easy recipe that is sure to please the seafood lovers.*

## Ingredients

½ cup flour
½ cup butter or oil
1 cup onion, chopped
¾ cup green pepper, chopped
¾ cup celery, chopped
2 tablespoons garlic, minced
1 6-ounce can tomato paste
3 quarts of water or chicken stock
3 teaspoons Cajun Sensation Spice Blend (page 10)

1 tablespoon Italian seasoning or dry oregano
1 tablespoon kosher salt
1 10-ounce package frozen okra, thawed
2 pounds peeled, raw shrimp
1 pound crabmeat, cartilage removed
1 pint oysters with liquid
Filé powder
4 cups cooked rice

Stove top

**1.** In a skillet over medium heat, make a medium brown roux with the butter or oil and flour. Transfer roux to a large pot. Add onion, pepper, celery, and garlic and cook until soft.

**2.** Add tomato paste, water or stock, and spices. Turn heat to low and cook for 1 hour.

**3.** While gumbo is cooking, drain okra and cook in a skillet until all liquid is almost gone, then add to the simmering gumbo.

**4.** Just before serving, add seafood and cook until shrimp are pink.

**5.** Place a half cup of cooked rice in the bottom of a bowl and spoon gumbo on top. Sprinkle with a small amount of filé powder before serving.

*Chef's secret: When cooking soups and stews, adjust seasonings again before serving; sometimes dry herbs lose flavor when cooked for a long period of time.*

### Shopping List

| | |
|---|---|
| all-purpose flour | Cajun Sensation Spice Blend |
| butter or oil | Italian seasoning or dry oregano |
| onion | kosher salt |
| green pepper | 10-ounce package frozen okra |
| celery | peeled, raw shrimp |
| garlic | crabmeat |
| tomato paste | oysters with liquid |
| chicken stock (optional) | filé powder |
| | rice |

# Washday Red Beans

### Serves 6

Red beans and rice are typically made on Mondays, which is also washday. Cajuns were resourceful, and making a long-cooking dish and doing chores at the same time was considered being "in the bonus." At our house, Mama made red beans with the leftover ham bone from Sunday dinner. This recipe is made from dried beans; however, canned beans could be substituted.

## Ingredients

| | | | |
|---|---|---|---|
| 1 | pound dry red kidney beans | 1 | teaspoon black pepper |
| 1 | cup onion, diced | 1 | pound smoked sausage or Andouille sausage, diced |
| 1 | cup celery, diced | | |
| ½ | cup green pepper, diced | 6 | cups cooked white or brown rice |
| 1 | tablespoon garlic, minced | | |
| 2 | teaspoons kosher salt | 1 | cup shredded cheese of choice |

**Stove top**

**1.** Rinse and soak red beans overnight. If there's no time for soaking, place beans in a large pot and cover with water. Bring to a boil and cook over medium heat, boiling for 10 minutes. Turn heat off and let sit for one hour, then proceed with recipe.

**2.** Drain beans and place in a large pot. Add enough water to cover the beans by two inches.

**3.** Add vegetables, spices, and diced sausage.

**4.** Cook for at least two hours, adding water as needed to keep beans covered.

**5.** Serve with rice and top with shredded cheese.

**To serve:** Serve with lots of hot sauce and crusty garlic bread.

*Chef's secret: For vegetarian beans, omit sausage or serve it on the side.*

### Shopping List

| | |
|---|---|
| dry red kidney beans | kosher salt |
| onion | black pepper |
| celery | smoked or Andouille sausage |
| green pepper | white or brown rice |
| garlic | shredded cheese |

# Donald's Jazzy Shrimp Creole

Yields 4-6 servings

*Over the years Creole cooking has merged with Cajun cooking to become what is served in the restaurants and homes in Louisiana today. Creole cooking is really a mix of different foods from the immigrants who moved to New Orleans. Tomatoes are often front and center for traditional Creole dishes, because of their abundance in the subtropical climate. My good friend Donald James, who used to own a restaurant in Minnesota, was always excited about Cajun and Creole food and often featured such dishes on the menu. This was a customer favorite.*

## Ingredients

¼  cup canola oil
1  medium sized onion, chopped
½  bunch celery, chopped
3  cloves garlic, finely chopped
2  bay leaves
⅛  teaspoon rosemary, crushed
Pinch of oregano leaves

1  28-ounce can whole tomatoes, chopped
3  ounces tomato paste
3  ounces tomato puree
Salt and pepper to taste
4  teaspoons sugar
1-2  pounds raw, peeled shrimp

Stove top

**1.** Smother onion and celery in oil (sauté covered) about 15 minutes.

**2.** Add everything else except the shrimp; cook slowly on medium to low heat for 45 minutes.

**3.** Right before serving, add shrimp and cook until pink.

**To serve:** Serve with white rice and garnish with chopped parsley.

*Chef's secret: Always remember when cooking tomatoes to add sugar; this improves flavor and balances the acid taste.*

### Shopping List

| | |
|---|---|
| canola oil | canned whole tomatoes |
| onion | tomato paste |
| celery | tomato puree |
| garlic | salt and pepper |
| bay leaves | sugar |
| rosemary | raw, peeled shrimp |
| oregano | |

# Donna's Crawfish Casserole

Yields 10-12 servings

*M*y sister-in-law, Donna, makes this dish during Lent. It was so delicious I had to have the recipe. It is very rich, and a little goes a long way.

### Ingredients

| | | | |
|---|---|---|---|
| 1 | 8-ounce package cream cheese | 1 | 10-ounce can cream of mushroom soup |
| ½ | cup (1 stick) margarine or butter | 2 | cups cooked rice |
| 2 | tablespoons margarine or butter | 3 | dashes white pepper |
| 2 | pounds crawfish tail meat* | ½ | teaspoon red pepper, ground |
| 1 | medium onion, chopped | 1 | tablespoon garlic powder |
| 1 | green pepper, chopped | 1 | 8-ounce package shredded cheddar cheese |
| 1 | 8-ounce package fresh sliced mushrooms | 1 | can fried onions for topping |

*  See page 211 for mail order sources.

Preheat oven to 350°F

**1.** Melt cream cheese and 1 stick butter together in a saucepan over medium heat; set aside.

**2.** Melt 2 tablespoons margarine or butter in a large skillet over medium heat and sauté crawfish, onion, green pepper, and mushrooms.

**3.** Add soup, rice, and cream cheese and butter mixture.

**4.** Add seasonings and pour into a greased casserole dish. Top with shredded cheese and fried onions and bake 30 minutes at 350°F.

**To serve:** Serve as a side dish for the holidays; it goes well with turkey.

**Chef's secret:** *Cover with foil before baking to keep the cheese from browning too much.*

## Shopping List

| | |
|---|---|
| cream cheese | canned cream of mushroom soup |
| margarine or butter | white and red pepper |
| crawfish tail meat | garlic powder |
| onion | rice |
| green pepper | shredded cheese |
| fresh mushrooms | canned fried onion rings |

# Creamy Artichoke Bisque

Yields approximately 2 quarts

*A*rtichokes lend this soup a tangy yet mellow flavor. It is traditionally served cold in most restaurants but can also be served hot with great success.

## Ingredients

| | |
|---|---|
| 2 | large russet potatoes, peeled and diced |
| 1 | shallot, minced |
| 1 | medium sweet onion, chopped |
| 2 | quarts chicken or vegetable stock |
| 2 | 15-ounce cans artichoke hearts, chopped |
| 1 | tablespoon garlic, minced |
| 1 | quart heavy cream |
| 1 | cup fresh mixed herbs—basil, oregano, thyme |
| | Salt and white pepper |
| ½ | cup green pistachios, chopped for garnish |

Stove top

**1.** Combine diced potatoes, shallot, onion, and chicken stock in a 3-quart saucepan or pot.

**2.** Cook until potatoes are tender, about 30 minutes. Puree potatoes in blender in small batches with part of the stock. Return the pureed mixture to the pot.

**3.** Add chopped artichoke hearts, garlic, heavy cream, and chopped herbs and mix.

**4.** Simmer for 30 minutes until desired thickness. Season with salt and white pepper. Garnish with chopped pistachios.

**To serve:** Serve with Cheese Pennies (page 44).

*Chef's secret:* Using an immersion blender saves time in this recipe.

### Shopping List

| | |
|---|---|
| russet potatoes | garlic |
| shallot | heavy cream |
| sweet onion | fresh basil, oregano, thyme |
| chicken or vegetable stock | salt and white pepper |
| canned artichoke hearts | green pistachios |

# White Bean and Lentil Soup

Yields approximately 1½ quarts

*Lentils are great little beans that cook fast and need no presoaking. Mix with canned white beans to extend the amount of soup and give it more eye appeal.*

## Ingredients

| | |
|---|---|
| 2 | tablespoons olive or canola oil |
| 1 | tablespoon garlic, minced |
| 1 | large onion, chopped |
| ½ | pound lentils (1¼ cups) |
| 1 | quart chicken stock |
| 1 | large jalapeño pepper, minced |
| 1 | 16-ounce can crushed tomatoes |
| 1 | 16-ounce can navy beans, rinsed |
| 1 | teaspoon sugar |
| | Salt and black pepper to taste |
| 1 | cup Parmesan cheese |

Stove top

**1.** Heat oil in a 2-quart saucepan over medium high heat. Stir in garlic and onion. Cook until soft.

**2.** Add lentils, stock, and jalapeño pepper and bring to a boil. Turn heat down and simmer for 30 minutes or until lentils are tender.

**3.** Add tomatoes, beans, and sugar and simmer about 10 minutes more. Add salt and pepper to taste and garnish with Parmesan cheese.

**To serve:** Serve with corn muffins.

*Chef's secret:* Beef broth can also be used for stock, as well as water.

### Shopping List

olive or canola oil

garlic

onion

lentils

chicken stock

fresh jalapeño pepper

canned crushed tomatoes

canned navy beans

sugar

salt and black pepper

Parmesan cheese

# Lenten Herbed Sweet Onion and Tomato Soup

Yields approximately 3½ quarts

*D*uring Lent, soup was a mainstay for a Friday night supper. This soup is delicious reheated the next day.

## Ingredients

| | |
|---|---|
| 1 tablespoon olive oil | ½ cup balsamic vinegar |
| 2 pounds red onions, thinly sliced | 2¾ quarts water or vegetable stock |
| 1 tablespoon garlic, minced | 1 16-ounce can crushed tomatoes |
| 1 cup celery, diced | 2 tablespoons fresh basil |
| 1 cup green pepper, diced | 3 large bay leaves |
| 2 tablespoons honey | Salt and pepper to taste |
| ¼ cup tomato paste | |

Stove top

**1.** Heat olive oil in a large Dutch oven or pot. Add onions, garlic, celery, and green pepper and cook for 10 minutes or until soft.

**2.** Add honey, tomato paste, balsamic vinegar, and water or stock. Mix well.

**3.** Mix in tomatoes, basil, bay leaves, and spices. Simmer for one hour to blend flavors.

**To serve:** Serve with a hearty Merlot and crusty French bread.

**Chef's secret:** *This can be a great base for baked onion soup—add cheese and French bread for a hearty dish.*

| **Shopping List** | |
|---|---|
| olive oil | balsamic vinegar |
| red onions | vegetable stock (optional) |
| garlic | canned crushed tomatoes |
| celery | fresh basil |
| green pepper | bay leaves |
| honey | salt and pepper |
| tomato paste | |

# Alligator and Andouille Sauce Piquant

Yields 10-15 servings

*Alligator season is the month of September in Louisiana. If you can't get down there to trap your own, you can purchase farm-raised alligator sold to local markets nationally by special order. If you find yourself ordering alligator, only order the tail meat and try to get it tenderized before it gets to you. Did you know that alligator has the highest calcium content of any meat or seafood?*

## Ingredients

| | |
|---|---|
| ½ pound butter, melted | 6 drops bitters |
| 2 cups flour | 6 ounces tomato paste |
| 2 cups onion, chopped | 1 lemon, sliced thin |
| 1 cup green pepper, chopped | Juice of one lemon |
| 1 cup green onion, chopped | 4 cups tomatoes, diced (fresh or canned) |
| ½ cup celery, chopped | |
| 3 tablespoons jalapeño, minced (fresh) | 1 tablespoon brown sugar |
| 2 tablespoons garlic, minced | 6 cups seafood or chicken stock |
| 1 teaspoon white pepper | 2 cups white wine |
| 1 teaspoon salt | 2½ pounds alligator meat, cubed |
| 2 bay leaves | 1 pound Andouille sausage |
| 1 tablespoon Pickapeppa sauce | 2 pounds whole mushrooms |
| | ½ cup chopped parsley |

**Stove top**

**1.** First, make a medium brown roux with the flour and butter in a large pot.

**2.** Add vegetables and spices and sauté until soft. Add tomato paste, lemon slices and juice, tomatoes, brown sugar, stock, and white wine. Simmer for 30 minutes.

**3.** Add alligator, Andouille sausage, and whole mushrooms. Continue to simmer for 45 minutes to an hour. Stir in parsley just before serving.

**To serve:** Serve with steamed rice.

**Chef's secret:** *This dish is better the next day.*

Note: Alligator meat can be ordered from one of the seafood sources listed on page 211.

## Shopping List

| | |
|---|---|
| butter | bitters |
| flour | tomato paste |
| onion | lemons |
| green pepper | fresh or canned tomatoes |
| green onions | brown sugar |
| celery | seafood or chicken stock |
| fresh jalapeño | white wine |
| garlic | alligator meat |
| white pepper | Andouille sausage |
| salt | whole mushrooms |
| bay leaves | fresh parsley |
| Pickapeppa sauce | |

# Snappy Chicken and Zucchini Sauté

Serves 4

*This is a quick and delicious stew that can be made in a snap with fresh garden vegetables.*

## Ingredients

| | | | | |
|---|---|---|---|---|
| 8 | chicken thighs, boned and skinned | 2 | medium zucchini, sliced | |
| 2 | teaspoons Cajun Sensation Spice Blend (page 10) | 5 | tomatoes | |
| | | ½ | cup chicken stock | |
| 1 | tablespoon olive oil | 1 | teaspoon Italian seasoning | |
| ½ | cup onion, chopped | 3 | tablespoons chopped fresh parsley | |
| 1 | tablespoon garlic, minced | | | |

Stove top

**1.** Rub Cajun spice on chicken. In a large non-stick skillet, heat olive oil to medium high heat. Add chicken and brown (about 10 minutes). Drain and set chicken aside.

**2.** Add onion and garlic. Sauté until soft (about 3 minutes). Add zucchini and tomatoes. Cook for 3 minutes more.

**3.** Add chicken stock and Italian seasoning, and return cooked chicken to the skillet.

**4.** Reduce heat to medium. Cover and cook about 10 minutes more or until sauce reaches desired thickness.

**5.** Garnish with chopped parsley.

**To serve:** Serve with brown rice.

*Chef's secret:* One 14½-ounce can of stewed tomatoes can be substituted for fresh.

## Shopping List

chicken thighs
Cajun Sensation Spice Blend
olive oil
onion
garlic
zucchini
tomatoes
chicken stock
Italian seasoning
fresh parsley

# Seafood and Fish

Louisiana is blessed with abundant waterways, rivers, and ponds. Since I grew up in the area near the Mississippi River, we often fished the spillways for crawfish. I will never forget the times we went crawfishing on Easter Sunday, which was sometimes the same day as the opening of crawfish season. I loved getting the nets out and ready. We always went after dinner in the afternoon. On one particular occasion, I brought along my prize treat of a large chocolate bunny in case I got hungry from checking nets up and down the bayou. Later in the afternoon, I went back to the car to get a bite of chocolate bunny only to find in horror that the bunny had melted on the front seat of my daddy's new car! The rest of the story is best left untold.

We often would have a sack of crawfish or a big "mess" of fish given to us by friends, and that's when we would sit for hours and peel, scale, or whatever else needed to be done to prepare them. My mama would carefully wrap them and freeze for future feasts. I think this experience of harvesting and processing quantities of food prepared me to become a chef. I was never intimidated by large amounts of food. It was always a good reason to get together with the neighbors, and it helped share the load of work.

Redfish was once an undesirable fish to eat, but as the popularity of seafood grew, it challenged fishermen to look for an alternative catch to bring to market. Now we are eating many more underutilized species than ever before. If redfish is unavailable in your area, fresh catfish, snapper, or any firm-fleshed white fish will substitute nicely.

# Redfish Arlene

Serves 4

## Ingredients

| | | | |
|---|---|---|---|
| 2 | pounds redfish fillets or other firm fish fillets | 1½ | cups heavy cream |
| 1 | tablespoon Cajun Sensation Spice Blend (page 10) | ¼ | cup dry sherry |
| 1 | cup all-purpose flour | ½ | cup shredded Parmesan cheese |
| ½ | cup canola oil | 2 | tablespoons fresh basil, chopped |
| 1 | bunch green onions, sliced thin | 2 | teaspoons kosher salt |
| 1 | tablespoon garlic, minced | ½ | pound crawfish tail meat |
| | | ½ | cup fresh parsley, chopped |

Note: If seafood is not available locally, see page 211 for mail order sources.

Preheat oven to 200°F for holding

**1.** Rinse fish and pat dry. Rub Cajun spice in and dust in flour. In a large skillet, heat canola oil on medium heat and fry fish until brown, turning once. Remove fish and keep warm in oven while making the sauce.

**2.** In same pan that fish was cooked in, drain off any fat and sauté green onions and garlic until soft. Add, sherry, bring to a boil, and add heavy cream. Cook for 30 minutes or until desired thickness.

**3.** Add Parmesan cheese, basil, and salt; cook until cheese is smooth.

**4.** Strain sauce with a large-screen strainer into a 2-quart saucepan.

**5.** Add crawfish to sauce and heat until warm. Spoon crawfish sauce over fish and serve hot. Top with chopped parsley.

**To serve:** Serve with fresh green vegetable in season and your favorite light pasta dish.

*Chef's secret: Chop parsley in large amounts and rinse under cold water in a thin tea towel. Squeeze water out and store in an airtight container in the refrigerator for up to a week.*

### Shopping List

| | |
|---|---|
| redfish or firm fish fillets | dry sherry |
| Cajun Sensation Spice Blend | shredded Parmesan cheese |
| all-purpose flour | fresh basil |
| canola oil | kosher salt |
| green onions | crawfish tail meat |
| garlic | fresh parsley |
| heavy cream | |

# BBQ Shrimp on the Bayou

Serves 6

*BBQ shrimp is a wonderful and simple dish. It is one of my favorites for entertaining friends and relatives. When I got married I served this the night before my wedding. Contrary to the name, there are no tomatoes or BBQ sauce involved in the dish itself. Fresh shrimp makes this dish extraordinary!*

## Ingredients

| | | | |
|---|---|---|---|
| 1 | stick butter | ½ | cup beer |
| 2 | tablespoons Worcestershire sauce | ½-1 | teaspoon red pepper |
| | Several dashes hot sauce | ½ | tablespoon kosher salt |
| ⅓ | cup parsley, chopped fine | 2-3 | pounds fresh shrimp with shells—jumbo works best |
| 1 | tablespoon garlic, minced | 1 | lemon, sliced |
| 1 | tablespoon sugar | | |

Preheat oven to 400°F

**1.** Simmer sauce ingredients for 5-10 minutes on medium heat.

**2.** Arrange shrimp in a shallow baking pan and pour sauce over shrimp.

**3.** Bake at 400°F for 10 minutes, turn off oven, and let stand at least 10 minutes before serving. Garnish with lemon slices.

**To serve:** Serve with crusty garlic bread sticks for a terrific first course.

**Chef's secret:** *Line your baking pan with foil for easy cleanup.*

## Shopping List

| | |
|---|---|
| butter | beer |
| Worcestershire sauce | ground red pepper |
| Louisiana hot sauce | kosher salt |
| fresh parsley | fresh shrimp with shells |
| garlic | lemon |
| sugar | |

# Hot Plate Crawfish Pie

### Serves 8

In *New Orleans, the term Hot Plate means daily specials. It could be anything and often was! Locals loved anything made in a piecrust.*

*Crawfish pie was invented to use up leftover etouffée. It is a staple today for Louisiana fairs and festivals because of its convenience. You could say it was probably "fast food" back in the old days, because it could be eaten on the run. We serve a smaller version of this for cocktail parties today. I like them because they can be done ahead and frozen. Although traditionally pie dough is used for this dish, we are using puff pastry sheets to make it easy on the cook and save time.*

### Ingredients

1   package frozen puff pastry sheets

1   beaten egg

**Filling**

1   recipe of Crawfish Etouffée, cooled (page 62)

Preheat oven to 400°F

**1.** Thaw puff pastry sheets as directed on box. Roll out on lightly floured surface. Cut circles of desired size—2-3 inch for appetizers and 5 inch for entrées.

**2.** Brush with beaten egg. Add filling and fold over, crimping the edges with a fork.

**3.** Brush again with beaten egg. Place on ungreased baking sheet.

**4.** Bake at 400°F for 15-20 minutes, or until golden brown and puffy.

**To serve:** Serve with lots of cold beer and plenty of Cajun music!

*Chef's secret:* A small saucer is a good guide to use for making entrée-sized pies.

**Shopping List**

packaged puff pastry sheets
egg
recipe of Crawfish Etouffée
(page 62)

Note: Crawfish tail meat can usually be found frozen in one pound bags at local markets. See page 211 for ordering crawfish or seafood from companies in Louisiana.

# Oyster and Eggplant Orleans

Yields 8 servings

*W*e served this dish at the restaurant for lunch during the height of oyster season. In Louisiana we used to serve oysters in the months that had an "R" in them. My guess is that these were cooler times of the year. With modern technology, oysters should be safe all year round.

## Ingredients

| | | | |
|---|---|---|---|
| 4 | large eggplants, peeled and diced | 1 | teaspoon kosher salt |
| 1 | large onion, diced | ½ | teaspoon white pepper, ground |
| 1 | cup celery, chopped | | Tabasco to taste |
| 1 | tablespoon garlic, chopped | 2 | pints of oysters, drained |
| 3 | eggs, beaten | 1 | cup bread crumbs |
| 4 | tablespoons fresh basil, chopped | ½ | cup Parmesan cheese, shredded |

Preheat oven to 350°F

**1.** Spread diced eggplant on paper towels. Sprinkle with salt and cover with more paper towels. Let sit for 30 minutes. This will take any bitterness out of the eggplant.

**2.** Sauté onion, celery, and garlic until soft. Add eggplant and smother (cook covered) for about 10 minutes. Remove from heat and let cool slightly.

**3.** Add beaten eggs, basil, salt and pepper, and Tabasco. Mix in raw oysters.

**4.** Pour into a lightly greased 2-quart casserole dish. Mix bread crumbs and shredded cheese and sprinkle on top.

**5.** Bake for 30 minutes at 350ºF until golden brown.

**To serve:** Serve with a green salad and crusty bread. This makes a tasty side dish for holiday entertaining.

*Chef's secret: Shrimp can be substituted with excellent results.*

### Shopping List

| | |
|---|---|
| large eggplants | kosher salt |
| onion | white pepper |
| celery | Tabasco sauce |
| garlic | shucked oysters |
| eggs | bread crumbs |
| fresh basil | Parmesan cheese |

# Catfish Pecan

Serves 4

I was lucky to grow up in a beautiful part of Louisiana. We had lakes and ponds very close to our house. I can remember spending many a summer as a kid fishing for catfish. It was here that I learned to live in harmony with some of the local snakes, possums, and other residents. The only thing that shortened our trip to the pond was not the wildlife, but the heat. But that just meant it was time to head home and do some "watering chores," including ourselves. Mama used to mostly fry our catch, but when I moved to New Orleans later, I learned there were "seven ways from Sunday" to prepare it. Here is one of my favorites.

## Ingredients

| | |
|---|---|
| 4 | 4 to 6-ounce boneless catfish fillets |
| ½ | cup seasoned flour (mixed with 1 teaspoon Cajun Sensation Spice Blend) for dredging |
| ¼ | cup canola oil and melted butter, mixed |
| 1 | cup pecans |

| | |
|---|---|
| | Juice of one lemon |
| 2-4 | tablespoons butter, softened |
| ½ | bunch green onions, thinly sliced |
| | Kosher salt and white pepper to taste |
| 2 | tablespoons fresh parsley |

Stove top

**1.** Rinse catfish fillets and dredge in seasoned flour.

**2.** Heat butter and oil mixture in a skillet over medium heat. Fry catfish until golden brown, turning once. Remove from heat and keep warm in a 200°F oven.

**3.** In oil mixture, add pecans and cook until toasted. Remove from heat. Add lemon juice and whisk in butter one tablespoon at a time.

**4.** Add green onions and parsley. Season with salt and white pepper to taste. Serve fish warm with topping spooned over each fillet.

**To serve:** Serve with baked yams and honey butter.

*Chef's secret:* Any firm, fresh fish will work.

### Shopping List

boneless catfish fillets

all-purpose flour

Cajun Sensation Spice Blend

canola oil

butter

pecans

lemon juice

green onions

fresh parsley

kosher salt

white pepper

# Warren's Browned Hard Fish for Company

Yields 4-6 portions

Whenever I visit home, my brother traditionally cooks something for me. It's a real treat for me because it's always something from the wilds of the swamps. On my last visit there, the weather was warm, so we had fish—one of his favorite catches to prepare.

## Ingredients

2   pounds firm fresh fish fillets

1   cup (2 sticks) melted butter for dipping

Cajun Sensation Spice Blend (page 10)

Stove top

**1.** Wash fish fillets and pat dry. If the fillet of fish is large, cut in 3 sections. Slice any thick fillets horizontally. The fish must be no more than 3/8 to 1/2 inch thick to cook properly. The fillets should not be too thick.

**2.** Using a fork, dip fillets in butter and sprinkle seasoning on both sides.

**3.** In a large non-stick pan or flat griddle, on medium to high heat, cook fillets, turning once. Fish will cook in about 5 minutes.

**To serve:** Serve with Cardiac Arrest Potatoes (page 159) or Pecan Basil Pilaf (page 166).

*Chef's secret:* Steps 1 and 2 can be done in advance and the seasoned fillets can be refrigerated up to 8 hours.

## Shopping List

firm fish fillets

butter

Cajun Sensation Spice Blend

# Des Allemands Catfish

Yields 4 servings

*F*ried catfish with hush puppies is the stuff that Cajun children of all ages dream about. Most abundant in Mississippi, catfish farms produce the most succulent and delicious catfish available.

## Ingredients

1 cup yellow mustard
3 tablespoons Tabasco sauce
2 pounds catfish fillets
1 cup corn flour, seasoned with 1 tablespoon Cajun Sensation Spice Blend (page 10)
1 cup milk
1 cup cornmeal
4 cups peanut oil (to fry in)
2 lemons, sliced
Tartar or cocktail sauce

### Stove top

**1.** Mix mustard and Tabasco sauce in a large bowl. Add catfish fillets. Marinate for 2 hours.

**2.** Season corn flour. Dip fillets in milk and then in corn flour, back in milk, and then in the cornmeal.

**3.** Deep fry in 375ºF oil until golden brown.

**4.** Serve with lemon slices and tartar or cocktail sauce.

**To serve:** Serve with hush puppies and sweet potato fries.

***Chef's secret:*** *To give the oil extra flavor, fry ½ cup onions in oil and remove before adding fish.*

## Shopping List

yellow mustard
Tabasco sauce
catfish fillets
corn flour
Cajun Sensation Spice Blend
milk
cornmeal
peanut oil
lemons
tartar or cocktail sauce

# Chef Donald James Oysters Rockefeller

## Yields 4-6 servings

*This is a classic New Orleans dish. If you can't be lucky enough to get oysters on the half shell, use the ones in the pint and omit the rock salt and shell part of the instructions.*

### Ingredients

| | |
|---|---|
| 1 small onion, chopped | ¼ teaspoon kosher salt |
| 1 stalk celery, chopped | dash of black pepper |
| 4 tablespoons parsley, chopped | dash of Tabasco sauce |
| ½ bunch watercress, chopped | rock salt |
| 1 cup butter | 1½ dozen oysters on the half shell or 2 pints drained oysters |
| ½ cup dry bread crumbs or cracker crumbs | |
| ½ teaspoon anise extract or pinch of ground anise | |

Preheat oven to 400°F

**1.** Sauté onion, celery, parsley, and watercress in 1/4 cup of butter over medium heat until soft. Remove from heat.

**2.** Stir in remaining 3/4 cup of butter, crumbs, anise, and seasonings. Set aside.

**3.** Pour a thick layer of rock salt in the bottom of a shallow baking pan. Dampen salt with a sprinkling of water. Pour liquid off each oyster in the shell. Cover each oyster, still in the shell with 1 tablespoon of crumb mixture. Arrange shells on salt and bake for 5 minutes. If you do not have

the shells, arrange drained oysters in a small baking dish and spoon crumb mixture over oysters in dish. Bake the same amount of time.

**To serve:** Serve with a crisp Chardonnay or sparkling apple cider.

*Chef's secret: Have your seafood shop prepare the oysters for you.*

### Shopping List

| | |
|---|---|
| onion | anise extract or ground anise |
| celery | kosher salt |
| parsley | black pepper |
| watercress | Tabasco sauce |
| butter | rock salt |
| dry bread crumbs or cracker crumbs | oysters |

# Carnival Pasta with Tomato Cream Gravy

Yields 4-6 servings

With *fresh pasta available almost everywhere, it has indeed integrated into the mainstream of Cajun cookery. In New Orleans, around the time of Mardi Gras, you can get pasta made in the three colors of Carnival—beet pasta for purple, spinach for green, and egg pasta for gold. You can substitute your favorite fresh string pasta in this recipe.*

## Ingredients

| | |
|---|---|
| 2 tablespoons butter | 4 tablespoons fresh basil, chopped |
| 1 tablespoon garlic, minced | ½ teaspoon kosher salt |
| ½ bunch green onions, sliced | ½ teaspoon white pepper |
| 1 cup Portobello mushrooms, sliced | 2 tablespoons lemon juice |
| 1 link Andouille sausage | 1 pound cooked crawfish tail meat* or shrimp |
| ¼ cup sliced black olives | 5 cups cooked fettuccine or other pasta |
| 2 tablespoons tomato paste | Chopped fresh parsley for garnish |
| 1 cup heavy whipping cream | |
| ½ cup Parmesan cheese, shredded | |

\* See page 211 for mail order information.

**Stove top**

**1.** In a large skillet over medium heat, melt butter and sauté garlic, green onions, and Portobello mushrooms until soft—about 10 minutes.

**2.** Dice Andouille sausage into small pieces and add to vegetable mixture. Add sliced black olives and mix well.

**3.** Add tomato paste and heavy cream. Stir well. Simmer until thick, about 30 minutes.

**4.** Add Parmesan cheese, basil, salt, white pepper, and lemon juice.

**5.** Stir in crawfish tail meat or shrimp and warm for 5 minutes on low heat. Do not overcook crawfish. Fold in cooked pasta. Serve hot and garnish with fresh parsley.

**To serve:** Serve with baby greens garnished with marinated artichoke hearts.

*Chef's secret: When cooking pasta, remember to salt the water and let it come to a rolling boil before adding pasta. A covered pot always cooks faster.*

## Shopping List

| | |
|---|---|
| butter | shredded Parmesan cheese |
| garlic | fresh basil |
| green onions | kosher salt |
| Portobello mushrooms | white pepper |
| Andouille sausage | lemon juice |
| sliced black olives | cooked crawfish tail meat or shrimp |
| tomato paste | cooked fettuccine or pasta |
| heavy whipping cream | fresh parsley |

# Summer Shrimp Boil for a Crowd

Serves 10

Boiled shrimp was always popular for family gatherings. Grand Isle is renowned for the best shrimp in Louisiana. Cajuns are fanatics about the "correct way" to boil shrimp. I have also heard of a method called "dry boiling," which means using the same steps and ingredients, but no water. Most recently, my brother shared one of his secrets to boiling seafood. There is a new product out called "Dump Boil" which is widely available. It is a mix of liquid and dry together. This eliminates the worry of correct quantities of dry and liquid. At the end of the recipe, I have enclosed the mail order resource for "Dump Boil" so you can say you have the real thing for your next shrimp boil.

Figure about one pound per person with shells on. If you can get the heads on, it's all the better, because you will be assured of freshness. Wash shrimp well before cooking. If you are lucky enough to know someone with a butane gas burner, you can cook outside. This works well when you have a large amount. An eight-gallon pot is ideal.

Setting up is easy for a shrimp boil: Just spread newspapers on the table and provide lots of paper towels or napkins and garbage bags. Set up a cocktail sauce station so everyone can make his "own" recipe of cocktail sauce. Have plenty of saltine crackers and cold beer on hand.

## Ingredients

| | |
|---|---|
| 10 | pounds shrimp, shell on |
| 3 | packages dry or "dump" crab boil mix or 4 3-ounce bags crab boil |
| 2 | pounds onions, peeled and quartered |
| ½ | 26-ounce box salt |
| 6 | lemons, halved |
| 1 | head garlic, chopped |
| 1 | tablespoon cayenne pepper |
| 5 | pounds small red potatoes, whole |
| 12 | ears corn, husked |

Address for dump boil:

Zatarains
82 First Street
P.O. Box 347
Gretna, LA 70053

(504) 367-2950
(www.zatarain.com)

Stove top

**1.** In an 8-gallon pot, bring 4 gallons of water to boil. Add crab boil, onions, salt, lemons, and garlic. Add cayenne pepper and simmer for 20 minutes.

**2.** Add shrimp to pot. You can fit up to 20 pounds at a time in 4 gallons of water. Turn off heat and let stand about 10 minutes until shrimp turn bright pink.

**3.** Remove shrimp and reheat stock. Add potatoes and corn and cook 10 minutes or until done. Remove vegetables and serve.

**To serve:** Serve with saltine crackers and cocktail sauce.

*Chef's secret: Shrimp can be served hot or chilled—so make a big batch!*

## Shopping List

shrimp, shell on

crab boil mix—dry or "dump style"

onions

salt

lemons

garlic

cayenne pepper

whole corn ears

small red potatoes

saltine crackers

cocktail sauce

# Crab and Shrimp Patties

Yields approximately 8-10 servings

*F*resh crab means summer in southern Louisiana. This mixture was traditionally served in crab shells that were saved from crab boils, and always served on seafood platters in the area restaurants. Today, they are still popular and served in a patty form.

## Ingredients

| | |
|---|---|
| 1 pound lump crabmeat | ½ cup celery, minced |
| ½ pound shrimp, cooked, peeled, and chopped | 3 large eggs |
| 4 cups soft French bread crumbs, no crusts | 1 tablespoon parsley, chopped |
| 2 tablespoons butter | 1 teaspoon oregano |
| 1 green pepper, finely chopped | ½ ounce Pernod liquor |
| ½ bunch green onions, sliced thin | Salt and white pepper to taste |
| | Tabasco sauce to taste |
| | Canola oil for frying |

Stove top

**1.** Pick cartilage from crabmeat. In a large bowl, combine crabmeat, shrimp, and 3 cups of bread crumbs.

**2.** Melt butter in a skillet and sauté vegetables; add to crabmeat mixture.

**3.** In a mixing bowl, beat eggs, parsley, oregano, Pernod, and spices. Mix until smooth and add to crabmeat mixture. Let sit for a few minutes. Add last cup of bread crumbs and stir again.

**4.** Heat a skillet with ½ inch of oil in it. Spoon mixture into frying pan to form patties and fry on both sides. Keep warm in a 200°F oven until all are done.

**To serve:** Serve with a spicy tartar sauce.

**Chef's secret:** *These are delicious with poached eggs on top for brunch.*

| Shopping List | |
|---|---|
| crabmeat | parsley |
| shrimp | oregano |
| French bread | Pernod liquor |
| butter | salt |
| green pepper | white pepper |
| green onions | Tabasco sauce |
| celery | canola oil |
| eggs | |

# Spottfair Jambayala

Serves 10-12

*I have named this dish after my good friend Pat Spott. I make it often for him and his lovely wife, Kay Biga, who entertain friends often in their grand, historic home in Duluth, Minnesota.*

## Ingredients

| | |
|---|---|
| 3 cups 5-minute rice | 1 tablespoon Italian seasoning |
| 6 cups water | 1 tablespoon sugar |
| 3 tablespoons butter or olive oil | 2 teaspoons Cajun Sensation Spice Blend (page 10) |
| 1 bunch celery, diced | ½ bunch parsley, fresh chopped |
| 2 yellow onions, chopped | 2 pounds large shrimp, raw (peeled and deveined) |
| 2 green peppers, chopped | 1 pound crawfish tail meat*, cooked |
| 1 tablespoon garlic, minced | |
| 1 28-ounce can diced tomatoes | |

\* See page 211 for mail order information.

Preheat oven to 350°F

**1.** Rinse rice and mix with water. Pour in a 2-quart casserole dish. Bake in a 350°F oven for 45 minutes to one hour or until all water is absorbed. Let stand for 20 minutes.

**2.** In a large Dutch oven, sauté celery, onion, pepper, and garlic in butter over medium high heat until soft, about 10 minutes.

**3.** Add diced tomatoes and juice, Italian seasoning, and sugar. Mix in Cajun spice blend and cook for about 20 minutes more on a low simmer.

**4.** Add parsley and shrimp and cook until they are pink and firm. Add rice and crawfish tail meat and heat gently. Serve warm.

**To serve:** Serve with an array of hot sauces on the table.

**Chef's secret:** *This can be made in advance and also freezes well.*

### Shopping List

| | |
|---|---|
| rice | Italian seasoning |
| butter or olive oil | sugar |
| celery | Cajun Sensation Spice Blend |
| yellow onions | fresh parsley |
| green peppers | large raw shrimp |
| minced garlic | crawfish tail meat |
| canned diced tomatoes | |

# Shrimp Mosca

### Yield 4 servings

*This recipe is shared by Donald James. It's simple to prepare, yet delicious!*

## Ingredients

| | |
|---|---|
| 2 | pounds shrimp, raw |
| 1 | whole head garlic, separated into cloves and peeled |
| ½ | teaspoon black pepper |
| 1 | teaspoon salt |
| 2 | whole bay leaves |
| 1 | pinch rosemary |
| 1 | pinch oregano |
| 1 | ounce olive oil |
| 1 | ounce white wine |

Stove top

**1.** Combine all ingredients except wine in a large, heavy skillet and sauté 15 to 20 minutes.

**2.** Add 1 ounce white wine and cook until the wine evaporates. Serve hot.

**To serve:** Serve with steamed rice. Use the cooked garlic as a spread for crusty French bread. It's delicious.

*Chef's secret: Medium shrimp work best for this dish.*

## Shopping List

raw shrimp, medium size
garlic
black pepper
salt
bay leaves
rosemary
oregano
olive oil
white wine

# Meat and Poultry

In the Cajun culture, beef was not as readily available as pork. Every year we used to travel to my daddy's hometown, Mansura, to attend the "Cochon de Lait Festival." They would dig pits and roast succulent baby pigs all day long. My daddy's favorite was "cracklins," which were the skins and meat deep-fried. We also bought our meat and sausage for the freezer and a bushel of sweet potatoes from the local farmers. Louisiana has many festivals where fruits of the sea and earth are celebrated. On our way home we would make our way to the French bakery in New Roads to stock up on "pistolettes" which are small, crunchy delicious rolls that I have never been able to find anywhere else in my travels. My mother would always make my favorite "Sunday Nite Supper," which was gumbo, pistolettes, and baked sweet potatoes.

This was her version of a quick and easy meal after a long day of travel to the country.

# Dizzy Steak with Creole Mustard

Serves 4-6

Flank steak's flavor is tremendously improved when marinated and cooked outdoors. The trick to tasty flank steak is slicing it very thin before serving. This is an easy do-ahead recipe that lets the host at a party spend minimal time in the kitchen with excellent results.

## Ingredients

2   1½-2-pound flank steaks

**Marinade**
½   cup olive oil
1   12-ounce can beer
½   cup creole or brown mustard
1   teaspoon kosher salt
1   teaspoon black pepper
1   tablespoon garlic, minced
2   teaspoons dry Italian seasoning

**Sauce**
2   tablespoons creole or brown mustard
1½   cups sour cream
3   tablespoons parsley, chopped
1   tablespoon honey
½   teaspoon kosher salt

Preheat grill to medium-high

**1.** Clean meat and trim any visible fat. Mix marinade ingredients and pour over meat; store in a sealed plastic bag. Marinate from 2 hours to overnight.

**2.** Mix sauce ingredients and chill for one hour.

**3.** Heat grill to medium high heat. Cook steaks for 15 minutes or until desired doneness.

**4.** After cooking, let stand 15 minutes before slicing. Cutting against the grain, slice thin and arrange on platter. Serve sauce on the side.

**To serve:** Serve with roasted potatoes.

*Chef's secret:* One flank steak weighs on average 1½ pounds and yields about 28 very thin slices per whole steak.

### Shopping List

| | |
|---|---|
| flank steaks | garlic |
| olive oil | dry Italian seasoning |
| beer | sour cream |
| creole or brown mustard | parsley |
| kosher salt | honey |
| black pepper | |

# Carnival Tenderloin Fillet
# with Easy Horseradish Sauce

Serves 10-12

*Roasting a beef tenderloin fillet can be daunting if one has not had the experience. However, I have found that the trick is to have the right pan. A large shallow roasting pan will do the trick. I always buy "peeled" tenderloins from the butcher and finish trimming them myself. I then take the trimmings (except the fat), run them through my Kitchen-Aid food grinder attachment, and make ground beef with it. This is one of my husband's favorite dishes. Cajuns get their resourcefulness from the French. They too have a habit of using "everything but the moo."*

### Ingredients

| | |
|---|---|
| 1 | 3-5 pound beef tenderloin fillet |
| 2 | tablespoons garlic, sliced |
| 2-4 | tablespoons coarse ground black peppercorns |
| 1 | teaspoon kosher salt |
| 1 | teaspoon Cajun Sass Seasoning Blend (page 11) |
| ½ | cup olive oil |

**Easy Horseradish Sauce**

| | |
|---|---|
| 1 | pint sour cream |
| ½ | cup mayonnaise |
| 2 | tablespoons horseradish |
| ½ | teaspoon dry mustard |
| ½ | teaspoon kosher salt |
| | Tabasco sauce to taste |

Preheat oven to 425°F

**1.** Preheat oven to 425°F. Using a sharp knife, cut small pockets in the beef, and insert garlic slices.

**2.** Rub the pepper, salt, and seasoning blend into the beef. Coat with olive oil.

**3.** Place fillet in shallow roasting pan and cook for 15 minutes. Reduce heat to 350°F and cook for 20 minutes more for rare meat. Use a thermometer—rare should read 125-130°; medium

should read 135-140°. The beef will cook 10 degrees more out of the oven.

**4.** Let fillet rest for at least 15 minutes before slicing.

### Easy Horseradish Sauce:

Yields 2½ cups

Mix all sauce ingredients and chill for 1 hour. Spoon over beef fillet.

**To serve:** Serve with roasted potatoes and baby green beans.

### Shopping List

beef tenderloin fillet
garlic
black peppercorns
kosher salt
Cajun Sass Seasoning Blend
olive oil

instant read meat thermometer
sour cream
mayonnaise
horseradish
dry mustard
Tabasco sauce

*Chef's secret:* To crush peppercorns, place on cutting board and crush with the edge of a small, slanted-side sauté pan.

# Steak Etouffée with Stingy Gravy

Yields 4 servings

*T*he smell of this recipe cooking brings back many childhood memories when I duplicate it at home. Meat and rice were staples in our house. I think it was our version of comfort food before it became popular. This dish typically has a long cooking time, but one can shorten it by using the pressure cooker or a slow cooker. If you have the time, the effort is worth the taste. The tougher the cut of meat the better.

## Ingredients

| | |
|---|---|
| 4 | tablespoons canola oil |
| 1-2 | pounds round steak, trimmed and cut in pieces |
| 1 | large onion, chopped |
| 1 | tablespoon garlic |
| | Kosher salt and black pepper to taste |
| 1 | quart of water |

### Stove top

**1.** Season meat with salt and pepper. In a large skillet, heat oil and brown meat, turning occasionally. Be sure not to overcrowd meat because it will steam instead of brown.

**2.** Remove meat after it is browned, add onions and garlic, sauté until nicely browned, and add meat back to mixture.

**3.** Add 2 cups of water and reduce. When reduced, add more water, one cup at a time. Repeat this process for about 2 hours until meat is tender. For pressure cooker or slow cooker, prepare steps one and two, place in cooker, and cook per manufacturer's directions. Gravy should be thin and dark after reducing. That's why it is called stingy gravy—there's not much there.

**To serve:** Serve with rice and glazed carrots.

**Chef's secret:** *Add one teaspoon of sugar to onions while cooking for extra flavor.*

## Shopping List

canola oil
round steak
onion
garlic
kosher salt
black pepper

# Regal Veal with Creole Mustard Sauce

Serves 4

*Creole mustard is a strong grain mustard with lots of flavor. In this dish, the sharpness is softened by the cream. It is a last-minute dish that is perfect for a romantic dinner for two. We used to serve this dish to our V.I.P catering clients who wanted something memorable.*

## Ingredients

| | |
|---|---|
| 1 | pound veal tenderloin |
| ¾ | cup flour for dredging |
| ½ | stick (4 tablespoons) butter, melted |
| 1 | large leek, sliced |
| ½ | cup red wine |
| 1 | pint heavy cream |
| 2 | tablespoons creole mustard |
| 2 | tablespoons fresh chopped chives |

Salt and pepper to taste

### Stove top

**1.** Trim veal and cut into 2-ounce portions. Dredge in flour and sauté in butter. Set aside in a warm oven of 200°F.

**2.** Add leeks and cook for one minute. Add red wine and deglaze pan, adding heavy cream after one minute. Reduce heat and simmer until desired thickness; then strain.

**3.** Add creole mustard, chives, salt, and pepper. Pour over veal and keep warm until serving.

## Shopping List

veal tenderloin
all-purpose flour
butter
leek
red wine
heavy cream
creole mustard
fresh chives
salt
pepper

# Donald's Beef Acadiana

Yields 6 servings

## Ingredients

| | |
|---|---|
| 6 | beef fillets, 4 ounces each |
| Salt and pepper | |
| 2 | ounces vegetable oil |
| 3 | tablespoons butter |
| 6 | tablespoons pimentos |
| 6 | tablespoons green bell pepper, diced |
| ¼ | teaspoon black peppercorns, crushed |
| ¾ | teaspoon fresh garlic, finely diced |
| ¾ | cup sliced fresh mushrooms |
| 6 | tablespoons brandy |
| 12 | medium shrimp, peeled and deveined |
| 1 | cup heavy cream |

Stove top

**1.** Season fillets to taste with salt and pepper. Add oil to heavy pot and heat until almost smoking. Add fillets and brown on all sides, cooking to desired doneness. Remove from heat and reserve on warm platter.

**2.** Pour grease from skillet and add butter, pimentos, bell pepper, crushed black peppercorns, green onions, garlic, and mushrooms.

**3.** Sauté until bell peppers begin to soften. Add brandy and flame it.

**4.** Add shrimp and simmer until they begin to curl and turn pink.

**5.** Add cream and reduce until thick, when sauce coats the back of a spoon.

**6.** To serve, place fillets on six hot serving plates and place equal amounts of sauce over each fillet.

**To serve:** Serve with roasted potatoes.

***Chef's secret:*** *Have your butcher trim your meat and grind the trimmed meat for burgers.*

### Shopping List

| | |
|---|---|
| beef fillets | pimentos |
| salt and pepper | garlic |
| vegetable oil | fresh mushrooms |
| butter | brandy |
| green bell pepper | shrimp |
| black peppercorns | heavy cream |

# Chicken Sauce Piquant

Serves 8

## Ingredients

| | |
|---|---|
| 8 | boneless skinless chicken breasts |
| ¼ | cup canola oil |
| 1½ | cups onion, chopped |
| 1 | cup celery, chopped |
| 1 | cup green pepper, chopped |
| 1 | bunch green onion, chopped |
| 1 | tablespoon garlic, minced |
| ⅓ | cup dry roux (page 7) |
| 1 | 15-ounce can tomatoes, crushed |
| 4 | cups water |
| 2 | tablespoons tomato paste |
| ¼ | cup fresh lemon juice |
| 3 | bay leaves |
| 1 | tablespoon Cajun Sensation Spice Blend (page 10) |

Stove top

**1.** Heat oil in large Dutch oven and brown chicken breasts. Remove and keep warm.

**2.** Sauté onion, celery, green pepper, green onion, and garlic until soft. Add dry roux and mix well. Add tomatoes, water, tomato paste, lemon juice, bay leaves, and spice blend.

**3.** Place chicken back into sauce and simmer slowly for 30 minutes. Serve hot.

**To serve:** Serve with steamed rice and French bread.

*Chef's secret:* *After chicken is done, let stand for 20 minutes. Adjust seasonings if needed.*

## Shopping List

boneless, skinless, chicken breasts
canola oil
onion
celery
green pepper
green onion
garlic
dry roux
canned tomatoes
tomato paste
lemon juice
bay leaves
Cajun Sensation Spice Blend

# Honey Pecan Chicken Fingers

### Serves 4

*This recipe is definitely finger licking good! Fried chicken was always picnic food for us along with potato salad and Mama's brownies. We always ate a very early lunch because we just could not wait!*

## Ingredients

4    boneless skinless chicken breasts
3    eggs, beaten
2    cups flour, seasoned with salt and black pepper
1    quart canola oil for frying
½    cup honey
½    cup pecan pieces

## Stove top

**1.** Cut each breast into 6 strips. Dredge in egg wash and then in seasoned flour.

**2.** Fry in oil until golden brown.

**3.** Melt honey in microwave for one minute. Drizzle over chicken strips while still warm.

**4.** Sprinkle with pecan pieces.

**To serve:** Serve with honey mustard dipping sauce.

**Chef's secret:** *This can be done also with bone-in chicken pieces.*

## Shopping List

boneless, skinless chicken breasts
eggs
seasoned flour
canola oil
honey
pecan pieces

# Stuffed Chicken Breast Jezebel

Yields 6 servings

A stuffed chicken breast is a great holiday dish that is easy and elegant. We served this in the restaurant where I worked as a chef in New Orleans. Crabmeat, shrimp, or crawfish can be substituted in the stuffing. This stuffing could also be used for stuffing turkeys at holiday time. They can be prepared ahead and cooked at the last minute.

## Ingredients

6   boneless chicken breasts with skin on

**Stuffing**

6   tablespoons butter, divided
½   cup onion, diced
2   ribs celery, diced small
2   cloves garlic, chopped
3   cups crumbled cornbread
1   cup cooked small bay shrimp
½   teaspoon poultry seasoning
½   teaspoon dried thyme
1   cup chicken stock or broth
Kosher salt and black pepper to taste

**Jezebel Sauce**

1   12-ounce jar orange marmalade
1   10-ounce jar pepper jelly
1   9-ounce jar Dijon mustard
1   8-ounce jar horseradish
Kosher salt and white pepper to taste

Preheat oven to 350°F

**1.** Wash chicken, pat dry, and set aside. Melt 2 tablespoons of butter over medium heat and sauté onion, celery, and garlic.

**2.** Add cornbread, shrimp, and seasonings. Remove from heat and add 2 tablespoons of butter and chicken stock a little at a time to reach stuffing consistency.

**3.** To stuff breasts, pull skin away from breast and stuff mixture under the skin, tucking point of breast under. Melt remaining butter and brush on before cooking.

**4.** Bake at 350ºF for 30 minutes or until golden brown. Serve with Jezebel Sauce on the side.

### Jezebel Sauce:

Mix all ingredients in food processor or mixer. Keeps for months in the refrigerator.

**To serve:** Chicken can also be served with a simple red pepper sauce: Puree 1 cup roasted red peppers with 1 cup of chicken stock in a blender and heat. Season and serve.

## Shopping List

| | |
|---|---|
| boneless chicken breasts with skin on | chicken stock or broth |
| butter | kosher salt |
| onion | black pepper |
| celery | orange marmalade |
| garlic | pepper jelly |
| cornbread | Dijon mustard |
| small bay shrimp | horseradish |
| poultry seasoning | white pepper |
| dried thyme | |

*Chef's secret: Packaged cornbread stuffing can be substituted in this recipe.*

# Panned Chicken with Brandy Cream

Serves 4

## Ingredients

| | |
|---|---|
| 4 | boneless, skinless whole chicken breasts |
| 1 | teaspoon Cajun Sensation Spice Blend (page 10) |
| ¾ | cup flour |
| 2 | tablespoons olive oil |
| 2 | tablespoon shallots, minced |
| 1 | teaspoon garlic, minced |
| 8 | ounces sliced mushrooms |
| 1 | tablespoon fresh herbs such as thyme, chives, oregano, chopped |
| 1½ | cups heavy cream |
| ¼ | cup Gorgonzola or blue-veined cheese |
| 4 | tablespoons brandy |

Kosher salt and white pepper to taste

Stove top

**1.** Wash chicken breasts and pat dry. Pound breasts between plastic wrap and cut in half.

**2.** Add seasoning blend to flour and dredge chicken in flour. Heat oil in large skillet on medium high heat and brown chicken. When done, remove and keep warm.

**3.** In the same skillet, sauté shallots, garlic, and mushrooms until soft. Add herbs and heavy cream. Lower heat and cook for about 20 minutes until cream is slightly reduced. Add cheese and brandy. Pour sauce over warm chicken and serve hot.

**To serve:** Serve with lightly buttered pasta and focaccia bread.

***Chef's secret:*** *Green onions can be substituted for shallots.*

## Shopping List

boneless, skinless chicken breasts

Cajun Sensation Spice Blend

all-purpose flour

olive oil

shallots

garlic

mushrooms

fresh herbs—thyme, chives, oregano

heavy cream

Gorgonzola or other blue-veined cheese

brandy

kosher salt

white pepper

# Grand Isle Duck Breast

Serves 4

My brother, Warren, starred in a video called "The Duckmen" which discusses the finer points of duck hunting in the swamps of Louisiana. Although the production was several years ago, he still signs autographs at the Ducks Unlimited shows. This is one of his favorite dishes to make for company. Simple could not describe it any better.

## Ingredients

4   whole duck breasts, boneless and skinless, cut in half
8   strips bacon
1   cup apricot jam
Salt and pepper to taste

**Chef's secret:** *Bacon can be precooked for a few minutes before wrapping.*

Preheat grill to medium

**1.** Wash and pat breasts dry. Wrap each piece of duck breast in bacon and secure with toothpick.

**2.** Cook breasts on medium heat, covered, on outdoor grill for 15 minutes or until done.

**3.** Melt apricot jam in a small saucepan. Brush on jam during the last five minutes of cooking.

**To serve:** Serve with Roasted Sweet Potatoes (page 161).

## Shopping List

whole duck breasts, boneless and skinless, cut in half
bacon strips
apricot jam
salt
pepper
toothpicks

# Rosemary for Remembrance Hens

### Serves 6

*One of my first jobs was as a chef at a large convention center in Baton Rouge. I served Cornish hens by the thousands. Over the years the recipe has stayed the same—very simple and basic. However, later on I developed a relish to go with it to give it a little jazz.*

## Ingredients

3   24-ounce whole Cornish hens

**Marinade**
½   cup olive oil
¼   cup lemon juice
4   sprigs rosemary, cleaned and chopped
1   tablespoon garlic, chopped
1   tablespoon kosher salt
1   tablespoon Cajun Sass Seasoning Blend (page 11)

**Relish**
½   fresh pineapple, peeled and diced small
½   sweet red pepper, diced small
½   bunch green onions, sliced thin
2   ribs celery, diced small
1   tablespoon canola oil
2   tablespoons orange juice
1   tablespoon chopped cilantro or parsley

Preheat grill to medium

**1.** Wash and split hens. Mix marinade ingredients and marinate for 2 hours to overnight.

**2.** Grill over medium heat, covered, for approximately 45 minutes.

**3.** While hens are cooking, mix ingredients for relish and let stand for 15 minutes before serving.

**To serve:** Serve with Dirty Rice (page 158).

*Chef's secret: Papaya or oranges can be substituted for pineapple in the relish.*

### Shopping List

| | |
|---|---|
| whole Cornish hens | fresh pineapple |
| olive oil | sweet red pepper |
| lemon juice | green onions |
| fresh rosemary | celery |
| garlic | canola oil |
| kosher salt | orange juice |
| Cajun Sass Seasoning Blend | cilantro or parsley |

# Andouille Stuffed Mirlitons

## Serves 6

*Mirlitons are widely available in most supermarkets. Other names are vegetable pears or Chayote squash. They are a basic staple to the Cajun diet, almost like cabbage, but there's no smell when it's being cooked. The most popular technique of cooking mirlitons is stuffing. You don't see stuffed mirlitons too often in restaurants, though. It is mostly cooked in the home.*

### Ingredients

| | |
|---|---|
| 6 mirlitons | ½ cup bread crumbs |
| 4 strips bacon | 1 egg, beaten |
| 1 onion, chopped | Hot sauce to taste |
| 2 ribs celery, chopped | 2 teaspoons kosher salt |
| ½ green pepper, chopped | 1 tablespoon dry Italian seasoning |
| 1 tablespoon garlic, minced | Extra bread crumbs and grated Parmesan cheese for topping |
| 1 pound Andouille sausage, chopped small | |
| 4 tablespoons butter or margarine, melted | |

Preheat oven to 350°F

**1.** Boil mirlitons until tender, about 1 hour. Fry bacon and remove, reserving fat.

**2.** Sauté vegetables in bacon fat over medium heat and cook until soft. Add Andouille and melted butter.

**3.** Add bread crumbs and beaten egg; mix well.

**4.** When mirlitons are cool, slice lengthwise. Remove seeds and scoop out insides, leaving some meat in the shell. Chop mirliton meat and add to above mixture. Add spices.

**5.** Stuff shells with mixture and top with extra crumbs and Parmesan cheese. Bake in 350ºF oven for approximately 30 minutes or until tops turn brown.

**To serve:** Serve with a side of buttered noodles.

***Chef's secret:*** *1 cup of cooked rice can be added to the mix as well.*

### Shopping List

| | |
|---|---|
| whole mirlitons | butter or margarine |
| bacon | bread crumbs |
| onion | eggs |
| celery | Louisiana hot sauce |
| green pepper | kosher salt |
| garlic | dry Italian seasoning |
| Andouille sausage | Parmesan cheese |

# Grilled Pork Tenderloin with Orange Shallot Glaze

Yields 6 portions

*P*ork *is very popular among the locals in Louisiana. This version has a taste of the "old South" with a sweet, tangy sauce. Pork tenderloin has the least fat of most pork products. I have made this dish on television for a summer program.*

## Ingredients

### Grilled Pork Tenderloin

| | |
|---|---|
| 1½ | pounds pork tenderloin, trimmed |
| 3 | teaspoons Cajun Sensation Spice Blend (page 10) |
| 4 | tablespoons olive oil |
| 2 | tablespoons garlic, minced |

### Glaze

| | |
|---|---|
| 2 | cups ketchup or chili sauce |
| ½ | cup orange marmalade |
| 3 | tablespoons honey |
| 2 | tablespoons balsamic vinegar |
| 1½ | teaspoons Worcestershire sauce |
| 1 | teaspoon seasoned salt |
| 2 | tablespoons shallots, chopped fine |
| 1 | teaspoon dry mustard |

Heat grill to medium high

**Tenderloin:**

**1.** Trim any visible fat from tenderloin. Rub spice blend into tenderloin and coat with olive oil and garlic. Marinate 2 hours to overnight.

**2.** Over direct heat of a medium high grill, cook meat for 4-6 minutes on each side or until nicely browned. Internal temperature should reach 155°F. Brush with glaze when almost done. Serve extra glaze on the side.

**Glaze:**

**1.** Mix ingredients together.

**2.** Bring to a boil over medium heat. Stir and simmer for 5 minutes.

**To serve:** Serve with potato salad and cole slaw.

*Chef's secret: Be sure to let any roasted meat stand at least 10 minutes before serving.*

| Shopping List | |
|---|---|
| pork tenderloin | honey |
| Cajun Sensation Spice Blend | balsamic vinegar |
| olive oil | Worcestershire sauce |
| garlic | seasoned salt |
| ketchup or chili sauce | shallots |
| orange marmalade | dry mustard |

# Cochon Du Lait

Serves 6-8

## Ingredients

| | |
|---|---|
| 4 | pounds pork tenderloin |
| 2 | tablespoons Cajun Sensation Spice Blend (page 10) |
| 2 | tablespoons olive oil |
| 2 | tablespoons garlic, minced |
| 4 | tablespoons fresh parsley, chopped |
| 3 | tablespoons fresh rosemary, chopped |

Kosher salt and black pepper to taste

Preheat oven to 350°F

**1.** Clean any visible fat from tenderloin. Mix spice blend with olive oil and rub on roast.

**2.** Sprinkle garlic, fresh parsley, rosemary, and salt and pepper on tenderloin and curl tail under for even cooking.

**3.** Let stand to room temperature, then roast for 30 minutes or until thermometer reaches 150°F.

**4.** Let stand 30 minutes before carving. Slice thin and serve warm or chilled.

**To serve:** Serve with baked sweet potatoes in their jackets.

*Chef's secret: For leftovers, heat sliced pork in your favorite BBQ sauce and serve on small buns.*

## Shopping List

pork tenderloin

Cajun Sensation Spice Blend

olive oil

garlic

fresh parsley

fresh rosemary

kosher salt

black pepper

# Salads

So many of the great vegetables and fruits that make delicious salads are grown in warm climates. Among other products, Louisiana is famous for strawberries, peaches, tomatoes, and peppers. In fact the Pontchatoula Strawberry Festival is one not to be missed. Cajuns love competitions in food, and the festivals are the best place to show off one's talents.

Growing up we always had a bountiful table on Sundays. It was usually when the cousins came to visit, and Mama always put out her best spread. Since we had three gardens a year, there was always something fresh.

# Festival Salad

Serves 8-10

*Here's a wonderful salad recipe that celebrates our most important holiday, Mardi Gras. The traditional colors of Mardi Gras are purple for justice, green for faith, and gold for power.*

## Ingredients

| | |
|---|---|
| 1 | head romaine lettuce |
| 1 | cup radicchio lettuce |
| 2 | yellow tomatoes, sliced |
| 1 | cucumber, sliced |

### Festival Dressing

| | |
|---|---|
| 2 | tablespoons creole or brown mustard |
| 1/3 | seasoned rice vinegar |
| 2/3 | cup oil (half olive is good) |
| 1/2 | bunch green onions, sliced thin |

Kosher salt and white pepper to taste

No cooking

**Salad:**

Wash lettuce and spin dry. Place in salad bowl and garnish with tomatoes and cucumbers.

**Dressing:**

Yields 1 cup

Mix all ingredients together and pour over salad.

**Chef's secret:** *Red cabbage can be substituted for radicchio lettuce.*

## Shopping List

romaine lettuce
radicchio lettuce
yellow tomatoes
cucumber
creole or brown mustard
seasoned rice vinegar
oil
green onions
kosher salt
white pepper

# Confetti Cole Slaw with 1-2-3 Dressing

Serves 6-8

*Although my good friend Joan Strandlie introduced this dressing to me in Minnesota, I have since found out through talking to my Aunt Mae that it is a favorite Down South as well.*

## Ingredients

### Cole Slaw

| | |
|---|---|
| 1 | apple, shredded |
| 1 | tablespoon lemon juice for apple |
| 3 | cups chopped green cabbage |
| 1 | cup chopped red cabbage |
| 2 | medium carrots, shredded |
| ½ | bunch green onions, sliced |

Kosher salt and white pepper

### Dressing

| | |
|---|---|
| ¼ | cup white vinegar |
| ½ | cup granulated sugar |
| ¾ | cup heavy cream |

No cooking

**1.** Toss shredded apple with lemon juice, then mix with other slaw ingredients and chill.

**2.** In a bowl, combine vinegar, sugar, and cream. Pour over slaw mixture and chill until serving time. Add salt and pepper to taste.

The secret to this salad dressing is one part vinegar, two parts sugar, and three parts cream.

**To serve:** Serve with sandwiches for a tasty outdoor picnic.

*Chef's secret: Try raspberry vinegar in place of the white vinegar.*

## Shopping List

green cabbage

red cabbage

carrots

green onions

apple

lemon juice

white vinegar

granulated sugar

heavy cream

kosher salt

white pepper

# Marinated Creole Tomato Salad

Yields 10-12 servings

*I*f you can't get creole tomatoes, plum tomatoes will do nicely. This is a standard at outdoor picnics and BBQs throughout Louisiana because tomatoes are always a bumper crop.

## Ingredients

10  ripe creole or plum tomatoes, sliced

3   sweet peppers, sliced (a combination of red, yellow, and green)

1   sweet onion, sliced

1   cup pitted black olives

3   cucumbers, peeled and sliced

½   bunch green onions, sliced thin

### Creole Dressing

¾   cup half canola and half olive oil

¼   cup rice wine vinegar (seasoned)

1   clove garlic, minced

½   bunch fresh parsley, chopped

1   teaspoon creole or brown mustard

1   teaspoon honey

1   teaspoon kosher salt

½   teaspoon black pepper

Fresh herbs of choice

No cooking

**1.** Layer tomatoes, peppers, onions, olives, and cucumbers in a pretty shallow glass dish.

**2.** Sprinkle green onions on top.

**3.** Mix dressing ingredients and pour over vegetables. Cover and refrigerate for 4 hours.

**To serve:** Serve with Dizzy Steak with Creole Mustard (page 114).

**Chef's secret:** *Feta cheese can be added for an awesome Greek salad.*

### Shopping List

| | |
|---|---|
| creole or plum tomatoes | rice wine vinegar (seasoned) |
| red, yellow, and green peppers | garlic |
| sweet onion | fresh parsley |
| pitted black olives | creole or brown mustard |
| cucumbers | honey |
| green onions | kosher salt |
| canola oil | black pepper |
| olive oil | fresh herbs |

# Plantation Corn and Pepper Salad

### Yields 6-8 servings

*M*ake this salad with sweet early white corn; it is delicious.

## Ingredients

5   ears corn, cooked and kernels removed

2   peppers—red and green, chopped

½   medium sweet onion, chopped

2   medium tomatoes, diced

1   tablespoon Jezebel Sauce (page 124)

2   tablespoons olive oil

3   tablespoons fresh parsley

Kosher salt and black pepper to taste

No cooking

**1.** Mix corn, peppers, onions, and tomatoes and set aside.

**2.** Mix Jezebel Sauce, olive oil, parsley, and salt and pepper.

**3.** Stir into corn mixture and chill for one hour before serving.

**To serve:** Serve with grilled meats or poultry.

**Chef's secret:** *Cilantro can be substituted for parsley for that "south of the border" taste.*

## Shopping List

fresh corn

red and green pepper

sweet onion

tomatoes

Jezebel Sauce

olive oil

fresh parsley

kosher salt

black pepper

# Streetcar Olive Salad

Yields 3 cups

*Whenever I visit New Orleans I never pass up a trip to the Central Grocery to browse the shelves and take in the smells of history. I recently noticed a sign that said "Central Grocery Olive Salad—often imitated, but never duplicated." I had to agree; what I remembered from years ago to be olive salad had changed. This is my version of it, but if you want the real McCoy, you will have to take a trip. But, don't worry; my olive salad will pass for a good imitation.*

## Ingredients

| | |
|---|---|
| 1 | cup pitted large queen olives with pimentos, coarsely chopped |
| 1 | cup pitted black olives, coarsely chopped |
| 2 | ribs celery, chopped fine |
| 1 | tablespoon garlic, minced |
| 1 | teaspoon dry oregano |
| 1 | tablespoon capers (small ones work well) |
| ½ | cup olive oil |
| 1 | teaspoon Cajun Sass Seasoning Blend (page 11) |

No cooking

Mix all ingredients together and chill.

**To serve:** Serve with just about anything that needs a little zip.

**Chef's secret:** *This is delicious on grilled meats and mixed in with pasta sauces.*

## Shopping List

pitted large queen olives with pimentos

pitted black olives

celery

garlic

dry oregano

small capers

olive oil

Cajun Sass Seasoning Blend

# Fat City Tortellini and Andouille Salad

### Yields 12 servings

*F*at City is a section of Metairie, which is a suburb of New Orleans where a lot of Italians settled. Most of my aunts and uncles on my daddy's side moved here from what they call the "country," which are points north of New Orleans. Fat City boasts a well-organized parade route during Mardi Gras, and most of the suburban locals catch beads and doubloons here.

## Ingredients

1   pound bag frozen tortellini, cooked

8   ounces Andouille sausage, sliced thin

½   medium sweet onion, sliced

2   peppers (red and green), sliced

1   15-ounce can quartered artichoke hearts

1   cup Creole Dressing (page 138)

Stove top

**1.** Cook tortellini per manufacturer's directions.

**2.** Mix all ingredients and marinate for one hour.

**To serve:** Serve with baby greens and focaccia bread.

*Chef's secret: Summer sausage can be substituted for Andouille sausage for a milder version.*

## Shopping List

frozen tortellini

Andouille sausage

sweet onion

red and green peppers

canned quartered artichoke hearts

Creole Dressing

# Sunday Potato Salad

Serves 8

*My mother makes potato salad for every large family dinner; it is one of her trademarks. Complete with the sliced eggs and paprika, it is heavenly with the delicious BBQ squabs we eat regularly on Sunday. Although my version is a little different, it still brings me back to those dog days of summer.*

## Ingredients

6   russet potatoes, peeled, diced small, and cooked

1   cup mayonnaise (low-fat will work well)

3   ribs of celery, minced

4   hard-boiled eggs, sliced

¼   bunch green onions, sliced thin

3   tablespoons vinegar

Kosher salt and pepper to taste

1   tablespoon sweet red pepper, minced

2   tablespoons parsley, chopped

Stove top

**1.** In a large bowl, mix potatoes, mayonnaise, celery, 3 eggs, green onions, and vinegar.

**2.** Add salt and pepper to taste. Garnish with remaining sliced egg, sweet red pepper, and parsley.

**To serve:** Serve with gumbo.

***Chef's secret:*** *Mix the ingredients while warm so the dressing can soak into the potatoes.*

## Shopping List

russet potatoes

mayonnaise

celery

eggs

green onions

vinegar of choice

kosher salt

pepper

sweet red pepper

fresh parsley

# Waveland Crab Salad

Serves 4

We served this salad in a restaurant I worked at near Lake Pontchartrain. It was the specialty of the house and presents beautifully. Try this recipe for your next small special occasion lunch.

## Ingredients

| | |
|---|---|
| 1 | pound lump crabmeat, cartilage removed |
| 1 | cup mayonnaise (low-fat will work) |
| 1 | stalk celery, minced |
| 2 | hard-boiled eggs, chopped |
| 1 | teaspoon fresh parsley, minced |
| ½ | teaspoon dry mustard |
| 2 | teaspoons fresh dill |

Dash of hot sauce

Juice of one lemon

No cooking

Mix ingredients together and chill. Serve on a large glass leaf-lined plate in a mound with the following garnishes:

Carrot and celery sticks
Sliced boiled eggs
Radish roses
Sweet mixed pickles
Sliced cucumbers
Tomato wedges
Lemon slices
Assorted crackers

*Chef's secret:* This salad can be used as filling for sandwiches as well.

## Shopping List

lump crabmeat
mayonnaise
celery
eggs
fresh parsley
dry mustard
fresh dill
Louisiana hot sauce
lemon
carrot and celery sticks
radishes
sweet mixed pickles
cucumbers
tomatoes
assorted crackers

# Triple Bean Tuna Salad

### Serves 8-10

*Just because these items are canned, do not hesitate to prepare this spectacular salad.*

## Ingredients

| | |
|---|---|
| 1 | 15-ounce can kidney beans, rinsed |
| 1 | 15-ounce can garbanzo beans, rinsed |
| 1 | 15-ounce can black beans, rinsed |
| 2 | 6-ounce cans tuna in water, drained |
| ½ | bunch green onion, sliced |
| ½ | cup olive oil |
| 1 | tablespoon minced garlic |
| 1 | roasted, peeled red pepper, diced |
| 1 | 12-ounce jar pickled vegetables |

Kosher salt and white pepper to taste

No cooking

Mix all ingredients together and chill.

**Chef's secret:** *Make this with your favorite canned beans.*

## Shopping List

canned kidney beans
canned garbanzo beans
canned black beans
canned tuna packed in water
green onions
olive oil
garlic
red pepper
pickled vegetables
kosher salt
white pepper

# Voo Doo Chicken Salad

Yields 8 servings

## Ingredients

| | |
|---|---|
| 1 | cup celery, diced |
| 1 | cup fresh spinach, chopped |
| ½ | cup pickled or roasted red pepper, diced |
| ⅓ | cup fresh parsley, chopped |
| 1 | pound cooked chicken, diced |
| ½ | cup mayonnaise |
| 1 | tablespoon dry Italian seasoning |
| ½ | teaspoon dry mustard |
| ½ | teaspoon kosher salt |
| ½ | teaspoon white pepper |

No cooking

Mix all ingredients together. Chill for one hour.

**Chef's secret:** *Dark chicken meat tastes great in chicken salad.*

## Shopping List

celery
fresh spinach
pickled or roasted red pepper
fresh parsley
cooked chicken
mayonnaise
dry Italian seasoning
dry mustard
kosher salt
white pepper

# Garden Picked Squash Salad

Yields 8-10 servings

*Squash and zucchini are always in abundance from the gardens of Louisiana. This is a delightful and easy salad to prepare for a summer supper.*

## Ingredients

| | |
|---|---|
| 4 | pounds yellow squash, julienned |
| 3 | tablespoons parsley, minced |
| 2 | tablespoons dill, minced |
| 1 | tablespoon fresh basil, chopped |
| ½ | pint cherry tomatoes, halved |
| ½ | red onion, sliced |
| ⅔ | cup olive oil |
| ½ | cup raspberry vinegar |
| Dash of Tabasco | |
| ½ | teaspoon salt |

No cooking

**1.** Combine squash, parsley, dill, basil, tomatoes, and red onion. Set aside.

**2.** In a small bowl, whisk remaining ingredients and pour over vegetables. Marinate for 2 hours before serving.

**To serve:** Serve with grilled meat or salmon.

*Chef's secret: Fresh raspberries make a beautiful garnish for this salad.*

## Shopping List

yellow squash
parsley
dill
fresh basil
cherry tomatoes
red onion
olive oil
raspberry vinegar
Tabasco sauce
salt

# Carrot Copper Pennies

Yields 8 servings

*The bright color of this dressing resembles copper, and carrots cut in coin shapes make them appear like pennies. They were a favorite of my Aunt June.*

## Ingredients

| | |
|---|---|
| ½ | cup canola oil |
| 1 | cup sugar |
| ¾ | cup apple cider vinegar |
| 1 | 10-ounce can undiluted tomato soup |
| 1 | tablespoons Dijon mustard |
| 1 | tablespoon Worcestershire sauce |
| 2 | pounds carrots, peeled and sliced like coins |
| 1 | large red onion, sliced thin |
| 1 | green pepper, sliced thin |
| ½ | teaspoon cayenne pepper |
| 2 | tablespoons chives, chopped |

Stove top

**1.** In a medium saucepan, bring to a boil the oil, sugar, vinegar, tomato soup, mustard, and Worcestershire sauce.

**2.** Steam or microwave the carrots until tender. Pour the oil/vinegar mixture over the carrots.

**3.** Add sliced onion and pepper, cayenne pepper, and chives. Refrigerate overnight for the flavors to "marry."

**To serve:** Serve with Sunday dinner as a cold side dish.

*Chef's secret:* These last in the refrigerator about a week.

## Shopping List

canola oil
sugar
apple cider vinegar
canned tomato soup
Dijon mustard
Worcestershire sauce
carrots
red onion
green pepper
cayenne pepper
chives

# Creamy Broccoli Salad

Yields 4-6 servings

Broccoli salad is a tradition at outdoor picnics. It makes a tasty side dish for BBQ meats.

## Ingredients

**Salad**

| | |
|---|---|
| 1-2 | stalks broccoli |
| 4 | slices bacon, fried and crumbled |
| ¼ | cup golden raisins |
| ¼ | cup sunflower seeds |
| ½ | cup red onion, chopped |

**Dressing**

| | |
|---|---|
| 1 | cup light mayonnaise |
| ½ | cup corn syrup (light) |
| ½ | cup apple cider vinegar |

Stove top

**1.** Clean broccoli into bite-sized florets. Add bacon, raisins, seeds, and red onion. Set aside.

**2.** Mix dressing ingredients and toss with broccoli mixture.

**To serve:** Serve with anything that has BBQ sauce on it.

*Chef's secret: Pecans can be substituted for bacon bits.*

## Shopping List

broccoli
bacon
golden raisins
sunflower seeds
red onion
light mayonnaise
light corn syrup
apple cider vinegar

# Dressed Shrimp "Crowns"

Serves 6

*At Mardi Gras time, each parade club elects a king and queen for the year. Part of their duties is to attend numerous social events held between the Twelfth Night and Fat Tuesday. This shrimp dish looks like a crown and is served in honor of the king and queen at some of these events.*

## Ingredients

3-5 large shrimp per person— cooked, peeled, with tail left on

**Dressing**

1 cup olive oil

¾ cup lemon juice

¼ cup orange juice

2 tablespoons fresh dill

1 teaspoon honey

½ teaspoon salt

¼ teaspoon cayenne pepper

2 tablespoons diced pimentos

2 tablespoons sliced black olives

3 tablespoons chopped parsley (fresh)

### Stove top

**1.** Lay cooked shrimp on one side and make a lengthwise cut about ½ inch through the body of each shrimp. Insert the tail in the body of the next shrimp, forming a crown. Repeat until crown is desired size.

**2.** Place the crown in a serving dish.

**3.** In a mixing bowl, whisk olive oil, and lemon juice, and orange juice. Add dill, honey, salt, and pepper.

**4.** Spoon dressing over shrimp. Cover and refrigerate for 6 hours or overnight. Before serving, garnish with pimentos, black olives, and parsley. Spoon dressing over shrimp again before serving.

**To serve:** Serve with crusty French bread.

*Chef's secret: This dish is excellent for a family gathering or a first course at a more formal party. Jumbo shrimp are the easiest to work with for this dish.*

### Shopping List

| | |
|---|---|
| shrimp | salt |
| olive oil | cayenne pepper |
| lemon juice | diced pimentos |
| orange juice | sliced black olives |
| fresh dill | fresh parsley |
| honey | |

# Acadian Layered Salad

Yields 6-8 servings

This version of Seven-Layer Salad has a Cajun twist to it. The salad can be made up to 24 hours ahead of time, which always rates high marks with me!

## Ingredients

| | | | |
|---|---|---|---|
| 4 | cups Romaine lettuce, torn | ¾ | cup mayonnaise |
| 1 | cup broccoli florets | 2 | tablespoons rice vinegar |
| 1 | cup shredded carrots | 1 | teaspoon Cajun Sass Seasoning Blend (page 11) |
| 2 | eggs, boiled and sliced | 1 | tablespoon grated orange peel |
| 6 | slices bacon (cooked, drained, and crumbled) | 1 | orange (peeled and sliced) |
| 1 | cup grated Parmesan cheese | | |
| 4 | green onions, chopped | | |

Stove top

**1.** Place lettuce in the bottom of an 8-inch diameter bowl. Sprinkle with a little salt. Layer broccoli and carrots next.

**2.** Arrange sliced eggs and bacon over carrots. Top with ½ cup cheese and green onions.

**3.** Mix mayonnaise, rice vinegar, and Cajun Sass Seasoning Blend together. Add grated orange peel and mix well.

**4.** Spread the dressing on top of the salad, sealing the edge of the bowl. Sprinkle ½ cup of remaining Parmesan cheese on top and cover with plastic wrap. Chill for up to 24 hours.

**5.** Before serving, toss to coat the vegetables and garnish with the orange slices.

**To serve:** Serve with crusty bread and a light fruit salad for a summer lunch.

*Chef's secret: Most of these items can be bought prechopped for convenience.*

### Shopping List

| | |
|---|---|
| Romaine lettuce | green onions |
| broccoli | mayonnaise |
| carrots | rice vinegar |
| eggs | Cajun Sass  Seasoning Blend |
| bacon | orange |
| Parmesan cheese | |

# Mama's Cajun Sideboard

My ancestors came to Louisiana eight generations ago from France. They were from around Nice and the Italian border, which explains our olive skin, dark hair, and love for good food and the good life. Originally our family name was Bordileno, and when my relatives came to Louisiana they traded produce up and down the rivers to the Indians.

Well, the story goes, the Indians could not pronounce my relative's long name so they renamed him "L'homme de Coco," which means "man of the coconuts," since coconuts were one of the products he traded. The family and the name stuck through the generations; even a town was given the family name, Cocoville. And we've been proudly Cocos ever since.

# Fruity Bourbon Baked Sweet Potatoes

Serves 6

$A$s far back as I can remember my mother has served this dish every single Sunday, no matter what. Since Louisiana is a major producer of sweet potatoes I suppose she is doing what she can to support the industry.

### Ingredients

| | |
|---|---|
| 1 | 16-ounce can sweet potatoes, drained and cut into bite-sized pieces |
| 1 | 16-ounce can apricots, drained |
| ½ | stick butter, melted |
| ¼ | cup good bourbon whiskey |
| ½ | cup dark brown sugar |
| ⅓ | teaspoon nutmeg |
| ¼ | teaspoon ground cloves |
| Dash kosher salt | |
| 1 | cup chopped pecans |

Preheat oven to 350°F

**1.** Mix sweet potatoes and apricots gently and pour into a buttered 2-quart casserole.

**2.** Melt butter in a small sauce pan and add the rest of the ingredients. Pour over the potato mixture.

**3.** Bake at 350°F about 30 minutes or until the top is brown and crispy.

**Chef's secret:** *This is a great twist on the old favorite Thanksgiving Day sweet potato casserole.*

### Shopping List

canned sweet potatoes

canned apricot halves in light syrup

butter

bourbon whiskey

dark brown sugar

kosher salt

nutmeg

ground cloves

kosher salt

chopped pecans

# Maque Choux

Yields 10-12 servings

## Ingredients

| | |
|---|---|
| 10 | ears fresh corn (5 cups) |
| 4 | tablespoons butter |
| 1 | green pepper, chopped |
| ½ | medium sweet onion, chopped |
| 1 | tablespoon fresh basil, chopped |
| 2 | tomatoes, peeled and chopped |
| ¼ | cup heavy cream |

Kosher salt and white pepper to taste

| 2 | tablespoons parsley, minced |
|---|---|

Stove top

**1.** Cut corn from the cob, and scrape cob to get all of the juice.

**2.** Melt butter over medium heat in a large skillet and sauté green pepper, onion, basil, and tomatoes until soft.

**3.** Add corn, cream, salt, and white pepper. Simmer, covered, 10 minutes. Sprinkle parsley on top before serving.

**To serve:** Serve with roasted meats and game.

**Chef's secret:** *Crawfish tail meat can be added for an easy entree.*

## Shopping List

fresh corn
butter
green pepper
onion
fresh basil
tomatoes
heavy cream
kosher salt
white pepper
fresh parsley

# Dirty Rice

Serves 6

**D**irty rice is a way to use chicken parts and leftover rice. One of the best uses of dirty rice is to stuff meats and poultry. You can make it without the gizzards and livers, but it is just not the same.

## Ingredients

| | |
|---|---|
| ½ | pound chicken gizzards |
| ½ | pound chicken livers |
| 2 | bay leaves |
| 6 | cups water |
| ½ | pound ground pork |
| ½ | cup sweet onion, chopped fine |
| ½ | cup green pepper, chopped fine |
| ½ | cup celery, chopped fine |
| 1 | tablespoon minced garlic |
| 1 | tablespoon Cajun Sensation Seasoning Blend (page 10) |
| 1 | cup uncooked rice |

Stove top

**1.** Place the chicken livers, gizzards, and bay leaves in the 6 cups of water over medium high heat and boil 20-30 minutes until tender. Save the broth and grind or process the livers and gizzards in a food processor.

**2.** In a large Dutch oven, brown the ground pork and add the onion, green pepper, celery, and garlic; cook until soft.

**3.** Add spice blend and rice, mixing well. Then add 2 cups of reserved stock; cover and simmer for 20 minutes or until rice is tender.

**To serve:** Serve with cornbread and Fruity Bourbon Baked Sweet Potatoes (page 156).

*Chef's secret: Converted rice works best for this recipe.*

## Shopping List

chicken gizzards and livers
bay leaves
ground pork
sweet onion
green pepper
celery
garlic
Cajun Sensation Seasoning Blend
rice

# Cardiac Arrest Potatoes

Yields 10-12 servings

*This is a great recipe that my brother shared with me on a recent visit. It is a rich and delicious dish; a little goes a long way.*

### Ingredients

| | |
|---|---|
| ½ | pound bacon, chopped |
| 2 | large yellow sweet onions, chopped |
| ½ | medium green pepper, chopped |
| 5 | pounds russet potatoes |
| 2 | teaspoons Cajun Sensation Spice Blend (page 10) |
| ½ | cup water or more |
| 6 | slices American cheese |

**Stove top**

**1.** In an 8-quart pot, cook bacon and remove. Smother onions and green pepper in bacon drippings until clear and translucent.

**2.** Wash potatoes and leave the skin on; slice 1/4 inch thick.

**3.** Add potatoes to smothered onions and peppers. Add Cajun seasoning, cooked bacon, and water.

**4.** Cover and cook until potatoes are soft, adding water if needed. When they are cooked, cover with American cheese and let stand with lid on pot to melt cheese.

**To serve:** Serve with Browned Hard Fish (page 100).

**Chef's secret:** *DO NOT STIR potatoes after they are tender.*

### Shopping List

bacon
yellow sweet onions
green pepper
russet potatoes
Cajun Sensation Spice Blend
sliced American cheese

# Sassy Eggplant

Yields 6-8 servings

*This is delicious chilled on sandwiches, topped with a little olive salad the next day.*

## Ingredients

2   large eggplants
Kosher salt
1   cup Creole Dressing (page 138)
1   tablespoon chopped parsley

Preheat grill to medium

**1.** To prepare eggplants, wash and slice about 3/4 of an inch thick. Lay out on paper towels and sprinkle with salt. After 20 minutes, turn eggplants over and salt the other side. This will take any bitterness out of the eggplant.

**2.** Marinate eggplant in Creole Dressing for 1 hour. Grill on medium heat about 5 minutes on each side until marked. When done, place back into the marinade, top with chopped parsley, and serve.

**To serve:** Serve with fresh Mozzarella cheese and sliced plum tomatoes.

*Chef's secret: Vegetable marinade can be reused, but remember to always discard any marinade from poultry or meat after grilling.*

## Shopping List

large eggplants
kosher salt
Creole Dressing
fresh parsley

# Roasted Sweet Potatoes

Yields 4-5 servings

## Ingredients

5   large sweet potatoes, peeled and chunked
½   cup olive oil
Kosher salt and black pepper
2   tablespoons chopped fresh rosemary
1   tablespoon garlic, minced

Preheat oven to 400°F

**1.** Arrange potatoes in a 9 x 13 casserole dish.

**2.** Pour olive oil on potatoes and coat each piece well with oil.

**3.** Add salt, pepper, rosemary, and garlic; mix well.

**4.** Roast for 45 minutes or until potatoes are tender.

**To serve:** Serve with roasted meats; garnish with chopped fresh watercress.

*Chef's secret: Fresh chopped herbs can be stored in olive oil for up to one week in the refrigerator.*

## Shopping List

sweet potatoes
olive oil
kosher salt
black pepper
fresh rosemary
garlic

# Spicy Peaches

Yields approximately 2 pints

In *Ruston, Louisiana, the Peach Festival draws peach lovers from all over the state to taste the delights of this local crop. This is a good recipe for a Sunday afternoon.*

## Ingredients

| | |
|---|---|
| 2 | pounds fresh peaches |
| 2 | cups sugar |
| 1 | cup water |
| ½ | cup cider vinegar |
| 1 | teaspoon chopped fresh ginger |
| 1 | tablespoon lemon peel |
| 1 | tablespoon apple pie spice (ground cinnamon, nutmeg, allspice and cloves) |

Stove top

**1.** Peel peaches, cut in half, and store in slightly salted water to prevent discoloring.

**2.** In a large saucepan over medium heat, combine sugar, water, vinegar, ginger, lemon peel, and apple pie spice. Bring to a boil and add peaches. Lower heat and simmer for 10 minutes until peaches are tender. Let cool slightly. These are better served cold.

**To serve:** Serve with fresh corn and pepper salad.

*Chef's secret: You could preserve these if you are so inclined.*

## Shopping List

fresh peaches
granulated sugar
cider vinegar
fresh ginger
lemon peel
apple pie spice

# Rockefeller Soufflé

Yields 4-6 servings

$S$*pinach is a good host for many flavors. In New Orleans, you will see lots of Florentine dishes on menus and always flavored with a dash of Pernod for that extra zip.*

## Ingredients

| | |
|---|---|
| 1 | cup Cajun Cream Sauce (page 12) |
| 3 | eggs, beaten |
| 1 | cup shredded Swiss cheese |
| 2 | 10-ounce boxes frozen spinach, thawed and drained |
| ½ | teaspoon ground nutmeg |
| 1 | tablespoon Pernod liqueur (or ½ teaspoon anisette flavoring) |

Kosher salt and pepper to taste

| | |
|---|---|
| ½ | cup grated Swiss cheese for topping |
| ¼ | cup bread crumbs for topping |

Preheat oven to 350°F

**1.** Mix cream sauce, eggs, cheese, and spinach together.

**2.** Add nutmeg, liqueur, salt, and pepper; mix well.

**3.** Pour into a one-pound loaf pan and sprinkle cheese and crumbs on top.

**4.** Bake at 350°F for 30-45 minutes or until brown.

**To serve:** Serve with broiled fish and roasted potatoes.

*Chef's secret: Canned cream of mushroom soup can be substituted for cream sauce.*

## Shopping List

Cajun Cream Sauce

eggs

Swiss cheese

frozen spinach

nutmeg

Pernod liqueur or anisette flavoring

kosher salt

bread crumbs

# Crusty Okra

Yields 4-6 servings

I remember my mama making this routinely with fresh okra from the garden. The local rabbits also liked the okra, so we had to grow some for them as well.

### Ingredients

1 quart fresh okra
Boiling water
Kosher salt
½ teaspoon cayenne pepper
Yellow cornmeal for dredging
Oil for frying

Stove top

**1.** Wash okra well. Cut off stems and cut into ½-inch pieces. Boil for 10 minutes in salted water. Drain well.

**2.** Sprinkle okra with salt and cayenne pepper and dredge in cornmeal. Chill 30 minutes before frying so cornmeal can adhere to okra.

**3.** Fry in 1 inch or more of oil until golden brown. Drain on paper towels and serve hot.

**To serve:** Serve as a side dish or with cocktail sauce as an appetizer.

**Chef's secret:** Always either parboil or smother okra before adding to a dish; this will eliminate the "slime" which is really natural sugar.

### Shopping List

fresh okra
kosher salt
cayenne pepper
yellow cornmeal
oil

# Easy Cheddar and Broccoli Rice Soufflé

Serves 8

*This dish has been a tradition for as long as I can remember in our house.*

## Ingredients

| | |
|---|---|
| 4 | tablespoons butter |
| ½ | cup onion, chopped |
| ½ | cup celery, chopped |
| 3 | cups rice, cooked |
| 3 | eggs |
| 2 | 10½-ounce cans cream of chicken soup |
| 2 | heads fresh broccoli, blanched and chopped |
| 1 | 4-ounce can of water chestnuts, chopped |
| 2 | cups shredded cheddar cheese |
| Bread crumbs for topping | |

Preheat oven to 350°F

**1.** Sauté onion and celery over medium heat in butter.

**2.** Add the rest of the ingredients and mix well. Pour into a greased 2-quart casserole and top with bread crumbs. Bake at 350°F for 30 minutes or until bubbly and brown.

**To serve:** Serve with Honey Pecan Chicken Fingers (page 123).

*Chef's secret: Add crawfish tails or shrimp to this for a delicious one-dish meal.*

## Shopping List

butter
onion
celery
rice
eggs
cream of chicken soup
fresh broccoli
canned water chestnuts
shredded cheddar cheese
bread crumbs

# Pecan Basil Pilaf

Yields 4-6 servings

*P*ecans have become the "State Nut" of Louisiana. I always get a big care package at holiday time from the relatives, so I can enjoy them with my friends in dishes like this one.

## Ingredients

| | |
|---|---|
| 1 | tablespoon olive oil |
| 1 | tablespoon garlic, chopped |
| ½ | cup pecans, chopped |
| ¼ | cup fresh basil, chopped |
| 1 | cup long grain rice |
| 2 | cups of stock or water. |

Kosher salt and pepper to taste

Stove top

**1.** On medium high heat, in a saucepan, sauté garlic and pecans in oil for 2 minutes.

**2.** Add fresh basil and rice and sauté for 4-5 minutes.

**3.** Add liquid, bring it to a boil, then lower heat and simmer for 20 minutes until water is absorbed. Remove from heat and let stand at least 10 minutes before serving.

**To serve:** Serve with Browned Hard Fish (page 100).

*Chef's secret: Converted rice is the best choice for consistent results.*

## Shopping List

olive oil
garlic
pecans
fresh basil
long grain rice
chicken stock (optional)
kosher salt
pepper

# Rice and Eggplant Dressing

Yields 8 Cajun servings

*Rice dressing is very familiar to Cajuns. These days, the trend is to stuff deboned turkey with rice dressing for holidays. People order these delicious birds months in advance for the holidays.*

## Ingredients

| | |
|---|---|
| 1 | pound ground beef |
| 1 | pound ground pork |
| 2 | onions, chopped |
| 3 | ribs celery, chopped |
| ½ | green bell pepper, chopped |
| 4 | large eggplants, peeled and chopped |
| 1 | cup water |

Salt and pepper to taste

4 or 5 cups rice, cooked

Stove top

**1.** Brown meats and drain. Add onion, celery, and bell pepper and cook until onions are transparent.

**2.** Add eggplant and water. Cook until eggplant is thoroughly cooked and very soft. Add salt and pepper.

**3.** Add rice and mix well.

**To serve:** Serve with roasted duck breasts.

*Chef's secret:* Stir in chopped fresh parsley before serving.

## Shopping List

ground beef

ground pork

onions

celery

green bell pepper

eggplants

salt and pepper

rice

# Apple Smashed Sweet Potatoes

Yields 4-6 servings

*S*weet potatoes are sometimes referred to as the "Gems of the South" because of their versatility. Here is a quick, easy version that goes great with pork or ham.

## Ingredients

4  sweet potatoes, cooked in their jackets
½  cup applesauce
3  tablespoons butter, melted
Fresh grated nutmeg
½  teaspoon salt

Preheat oven to 350°F

**1.** Peel skin from sweet potatoes, place in a large bowl, and smash with a fork.

**2.** Add applesauce, melted butter, nutmeg, and salt.

**3.** Spread in small baking dish and reheat for approximately 30 minutes at 350°F.

**To serve:** Serve with chopped parsley for garnish.

**Chef's secret:** *Raisins are a nice addition to this dish.*

## Shopping List

sweet potatoes
applesauce
butter
nutmeg
salt

# Carrots Side Car

Yields 8 servings

*Carrots always seem to find a place on our holiday table. This is an old Creole favorite served alongside roasted meats on Sunday.*

Preheat oven to 400°F

### Ingredients

| | |
|---|---|
| 2 | pounds baby peeled carrots |
| ½ | cup butter, melted |
| ½ | teaspoon salt |
| 5 | tablespoons lemon juice |
| 2 | tablespoons brandy |
| 3 | tablespoons triple sec |
| White pepper to taste | |

**1.** Steam carrots; set aside in a large bowl.

**2.** In a small saucepan, combine melted butter, salt, lemon juice, brandy, and triple sec. Add white pepper to taste and heat over medium heat to a boil. Pour over carrots.

**To serve:** Serve with roasted pork loin garnished with orange slices.

**Chef's secret:** *These can be served at room temperature as well.*

### Shopping List

baby carrots
butter
salt
lemon juice
brandy
triple sec
white pepper

# Sweet Potatoes with a Sugar-Pecan Topping

Yield 6 servings

*Another winner by Donald James!*

## Ingredients

**Sweet potatoes**

1½ pounds red-skinned sweet potatoes, peeled and cut into 1-inch pieces (about 2 large)

6 tablespoons unsalted butter

1 large egg

6 tablespoons sugar

1 teaspoon pumpkin pie spice

Pinch of salt

**Topping**

1½ cups corn flakes, crushed

½ cup (packed) brown sugar

½ cup chopped pecans

6 tablespoons unsalted butter

---

Preheat oven to 400°F

**1.** Cook sweet potatoes in large pot of boiling water until tender, about 15 minutes.

**2.** Drain; transfer to large bowl and add butter. Beat with mixer until smooth. Add egg, sugar, spice, and salt; beat to blend.

**3.** Transfer to 8 x 8 baking dish. Bake potatoes until beginning to brown around edges and slightly puffed, about 25 minutes.

**4.** Mix together all topping ingredients. Spoon over potatoes and bake about 10 minutes more.

**To serve:** Serve with roasted meats.

---

**Chef's secret:** *Yams can also be used for this dish.*

### Shopping List

sweet potatoes

unsalted butter

egg

sugar

pumpkin pie spice

salt

corn flakes

brown sugar

chopped pecans

# Eggplant Etouffée

Yields 6-8 servings

*B*ecause the eggplant is a "nightshade" vegetable, it is related to the potato and tomato. Though thought of as a vegetable, it is really a fruit—a berry.

## Ingredients

| | |
|---|---|
| 4 | tablespoons butter |
| 2 | onions, chopped |
| 1 | green pepper, chopped |
| 2 | ribs celery, chopped |
| 3 | fresh tomatoes, chopped |
| 1 | large eggplant, sliced ½ inch thick (salt and let sit for 20 minutes) |
| 1 | tablespoons garlic, minced |
| 1 | teaspoon seasoned salt |
| ¼ | teaspoon Cajun Sensation Spice Blend (page 10) |

Stove top

**1.** Melt butter in a large skillet. Cook onions, green pepper, and celery.

**2.** Add tomatoes and cook slowly for about 30 minutes.

**3.** Add eggplant, garlic, seasoned salt, and Cajun seasoning. Cover and simmer for 30 minutes.

**To serve:** Serve with rice for a healthy lunch.

***Chef's secret:*** *Canned, diced tomatoes can be substituted for fresh.*

## Shopping List

butter
onions
green pepper
celery
tomatoes
eggplant
garlic
seasoned salt
Cajun Sensation Spice Blend

# Easy Southern Corn Pone

Yields 10-12 servings

I *don't usually go for canned or convenience foods, but this dish is foolproof and a hit every time I make it. It goes well with BBQ meats.*

## Ingredients

| | |
|---|---|
| ½ | cup butter, melted |
| 2 | large eggs, beaten |
| 1 | 16-ounce can whole kernel corn |
| 1 | 16-ounce can creamed corn |
| 1 | 8-ounce container sour cream |
| 1 | teaspoon dry sage, crushed |
| 1 | box Jiffy cornbread mix |
| 4 | tablespoons diced red pepper or pimento |

Preheat oven to 350°F

**1.** Combine melted butter, eggs, corn, sour cream, and sage in a large mixing bowl. Stir until well blended.

**2.** Add cornbread mix and diced red pepper and stir. Spread in a greased 9 x 13-inch casserole dish.

**3.** Bake for 45 minutes at 350°F or until brown.

**To serve:** Serve with roasted meats and a green salad.

**Chef's secret:** *Shredded cheddar cheese could be added for extra texture before baking.*

## Shopping List

butter
eggs
canned whole kernel corn
canned creamed corn
sour cream
dry sage
Jiffy cornbread mix
red pepper or pimento

# Ruston Peach Chutney

Yields 4-5 quarts

This is a great dish to use up really ripe peaches. We buy "seconds" at the farmers market to make this and "put by" for the winter.

## Ingredients

| | |
|---|---|
| 10 | pounds ripe peaches |
| 1 | large red onion, chopped |
| 1 | cup cider vinegar |
| 1 | cup dark brown sugar |
| ½ | cup golden raisins |
| 1 | tablespoon ground ginger |
| 1 | teaspoon ground cinnamon |
| 1 | teaspoon ground nutmeg |
| 1 | teaspoon ground cumin |
| 1 | large green pepper, chopped |

Stove top

**1.** In a large pot, heat 3 quarts of water to boiling. Poach peaches about 5 minutes until the skins start to remove easily. Remove peaches from boiling water and place in a large bowl. Cover with plastic wrap for 5 minutes to loosen the skins.

**2.** Peel, dice, and place in a large pot. Add chopped red onion, vinegar, dark brown sugar, raisins, and spices. Cook for 2 hours, add chopped green pepper, and cook for 30 minutes more.

**3.** Let cool and pack into freezer bags.

**To serve:** Serve with roasted meats or poultry.

*Chef's secret: Mix with cream cheese for a delicious spread.*

## Shopping List

ripe peaches
large red onion
cider vinegar
dark brown sugar
golden raisins
ground ginger, cinnamon, nutmeg, cumin
green pepper

# Desserts

Sweets always follow a family meal; the choices depend on what was eaten before dessert, as well as the time of the year.

Baking is becoming a lost art in today's fast-paced life, with some attention still given to it around the holidays. Louisiana fruits and nuts were always an inspiration in our house. Our holiday rituals would start in early November with spicy fruitcakes and cookies.

Cobblers, ice creams, and pecan desserts were always served, even after a large dinner. Mama always had something on hand just in case someone stopped by. We always enjoyed visits from neighbors as kids because that meant a chance to drink cafe au lait and eat sweets in the middle of the afternoon.

# Jazzed Pecan Pie

*This is a twist on a traditional favorite. Make two and freeze one.*

## Ingredients

| | |
|---|---|
| 1 | cup pecans |
| ⅓ | cup bourbon whiskey |
| 3 | large eggs |
| ½ | cup dark corn syrup |
| ½ | cup light corn syrup (mix syrups together) |
| 1 | cup brown sugar |
| 2 | tablespoons flour |
| 1 | teaspoon almond extract |
| 1 | pinch salt |

**Bottom layer:**

| | |
|---|---|
| 8 | ounces cream cheese |
| 1 | egg |
| ¼ | cup powdered sugar |
| ½ | cup Heath Bar brickle chips |
| 1 | 9-inch deep-dish pie shell |

Preheat oven to 350°F

**1.** Soak pecans in bourbon for at least 1 hour.

**2.** In a large mixing bowl, combine eggs, corn syrups, brown sugar, flour, almond extract, and salt.

**3.** In a small mixing bowl, mix cream cheese, egg, and powdered sugar. Spread at the bottom of the pie shell. Sprinkle brickle chips on top of cream cheese mixture.

**4.** Add pecans and filling. Bake at 350°F for 45 minutes to an hour until pie rises.

**To serve:** Serve with butterscotch caramel sauce and praline ice cream.

*Chef's secret: Soaking nuts in liquor before cooking always adds extra flavor in dishes.*

## Shopping List

pecans
bourbon whiskey
eggs
dark corn syrup
light corn syrup
brown sugar
all-purpose flour
almond extract
salt
cream cheese
powdered confectioner's sugar
Heath Bar brickle chips
9-inch deep-dish pie shell

# Grasshopper Pie

Yields 8 servings

*Cool and creamy, this dessert will make you look like a star.*

## Ingredients

| | |
|---|---|
| 1 | box chocolate wafer cookies |
| 1 | tablespoon sugar |
| ¼ | cup melted butter |
| 24 | large marshmallows |
| ½ | cup milk |
| 1 | pint whipping cream |
| 3 | tablespoons green creme de menthe liqueur |

Shaved chocolate for garnish

No baking

**1.** Crush cookies and add melted butter and sugar. Press in pie plate.

**2.** Place marshmallows and milk in a double boiler; melt and cool completely.

**3.** Beat whipping cream into soft peaks and add creme de menthe liqueur. Reserve ½ cup of mix for garnish.

**4.** Fold remainder into marshmallow mixture. Pour filling in prepared crust. Freeze for at least 3 hours or until firm. Serve pie garnished with reserved whipped cream and top with shaved chocolate.

**To serve:** Serve with fresh mint and chocolate sauce drizzled on the plate.

**Chef's secret:** *Line pie plate with foil and butter it for easy serving.*

## Shopping List

chocolate wafer cookies
granulated sugar
butter
large marshmallows
milk
whipping cream
green creme de menthe liqueur
shaved chocolate

# Blackberry Patch Cobbler

Yields 8-10 servings

*We used to pick blackberries every year to make delicious ice cream and cobblers. What I remember most is the heat and the mosquitoes, but we endured because we knew that the reward would be a mouth-watering cobbler for dinner that night.*

## Ingredients

### Filling
| | |
|---|---|
| 3 | pints fresh blackberries |
| ½ | cup sugar |
| 2 | tablespoons cornstarch |
| 1 | tablespoon lemon zest |

### Batter
| | |
|---|---|
| 1 | cup all-purpose flour |
| ⅔ | cup granulated sugar |
| ½ | teaspoon salt |
| 1½ | teaspoons baking powder |
| 1 | cup heavy cream |
| 1 | egg |
| 5 | tablespoons butter, melted |
| ½ | teaspoon ground ginger |
| ½ | teaspoon ground cinnamon |

Preheat oven to 375°F

**1.** Wash berries and dry on paper towels. In a large bowl, cover berries with sugar and add cornstarch, coating evenly. Grate lemon zest and add. Pour into greased 2-quart casserole.

**2.** In a mixing bowl, by hand combine flour, sugar, salt, baking powder, cream, and egg.

**3.** Add the melted butter, ginger, and cinnamon and stir. Top the fruit with the batter and bake 35-40 minutes. If browning too fast, cover with foil for last minutes of baking. Cool and dust with sugar.

**To serve:** Serve with an inexpensive vanilla ice cream melted to make a quick sauce.

*Chef's secret: Use butter wrappers to grease baking dishes.*

Note: You can use peaches, apples, or any other berry for this dish.

## Shopping List

| | |
|---|---|
| fresh blackberries | baking powder |
| granulated sugar | heavy cream |
| cornstarch | egg |
| lemon zest | butter |
| all-purpose flour | ground ginger |
| salt | ground cinnamon |

# Sweet Potato Pie with Quick Praline Sauce

Yields 8 servings

## Ingredients

| | |
|---|---|
| 2 | cups cooked and mashed sweet potatoes |
| 4 | tablespoons butter, melted |
| 3 | large eggs, beaten |
| ¾ | cup brown sugar |
| 2 | tablespoons dark corn syrup |
| 1 | teaspoon cinnamon |
| ½ | teaspoon freshly grated nutmeg |
| 2 | tablespoons rum (optional) |
| ⅔ | cup half-and-half cream |
| 1 | 9-inch pie shell |

**Quick Praline Sauce**

| | |
|---|---|
| 24 | caramel candies |
| 4 | tablespoons heavy cream |
| ¼ | cup pecans, chopped |
| 2 | tablespoons almond liqueur |

Preheat oven 375°F

**1.** Combine all ingredients in a large mixing bowl.

**2.** Partially bake pie shell for 5 minutes. Pour mixture into shell and bake for about 35 minutes.

**Quick Praline Sauce:**

Melt caramels in microwave for 1 minute; stir and add other ingredients. Cook for 30 seconds at a time until melted. Drizzle over pie.

**To serve:** Serve with cinnamon whipped cream.

**Chef's secret:** *Sprinkle pie with chopped pecans before baking.*

## Shopping List

sweet potatoes
butter
eggs
brown sugar
dark corn syrup
cinnamon
nutmeg
rum (optional)
half-and-half cream
9-inch pie shell
caramel candies
heavy cream
pecans
almond liqueur

# White Chocolate Bread Pudding with Raspberry Almond Crème

Yields 8-10 servings

## Ingredients

6    cups stale bread cubes
4    large eggs
1½  cups granulated sugar
2    teaspoons almond extract
1    quart of milk or half-and-half cream
½   teaspoon ground nutmeg
1    teaspoon ground cinnamon
¾   cup white chocolate chips
½   stick butter, softened

### Raspberry Almond Crème

½   cup heavy cream
½   teaspoon almond extract
¼   cup granulated sugar
3    tablespoons sour cream
1    teaspoon lemon zest
1    pint fresh raspberries

Preheat oven to 350°F

**1.** Tear or cut bread into small 1-inch pieces. Set aside.

**2.** In a large bowl, beat eggs; add sugar, almond extract, milk, and spices, and mix well.

**3.** Add bread to custard mixture, then add white chocolate chips.

**4.** Generously grease a 2-quart casserole dish with butter. Pour bread mixture in dish and bake for 45 minutes or until puffy at 350°F. Serve with:

### Raspberry Almond Crème

Yields 1½ cups

Beat cream, add extract, sugar, sour cream, and lemon zest. Add in fresh raspberries last.

**Chef's secret:** *You can substitue thawed, well drained frozen raspberries.*

## Shopping List

bread
eggs
granulated sugar
almond extract
milk or half-and-half cream
ground nutmeg
ground cinnamon
white chocolate chips
butter
heavy cream
sour cream
lemon zest
fresh raspberries

# Crème Brulée

Yields 4-6 portions

*Although Chef Donald James supplies this recipe from his collection, it is quite similar to the recipe we used in New Orleans.*

## Ingredients

4    egg yolks
¼   cup brown sugar
2½ cups light cream
1    vanilla bean or ½ teaspoon
     vanilla extract
extra sugar for topping

Preheat oven to 325°F

**1.** Place egg yolks in mixing bowl and blend in brown sugar with a wooden spoon until smooth.

**2.** Heat the cream and vanilla in a saucepan until warm, but do not boil.

**3.** Remove vanilla bean and pour cream slowly over the egg mixture, blending thoroughly.

**4.** Strain the custard into a buttered shallow 1½-pint ovenproof dish or individual custard cups.

**5.** Place in a baking dish of warm water and bake at 325-350°F oven for 45-60 minutes or until custard is set. Allow to cool.

**6.** Sprinkle a little sugar on top of custard and carmelize under the broiler. Watch carefully!

**To serve:** Serve with fruit and cream.

*Chef's secret: A propane blowtorch works wonders for carmelizing sugar.*

## Shopping List

eggs
brown sugar
light cream
vanilla bean or vanilla extract

# Mama's Brownies

Yields 24 brownies

*My mother is locally famous for her brownies. She has made them for weddings, bake sales, parties, and picnics. My Aunt Rena said once that she never knew a time that my mother did not bring food to someone when she was visiting. This recipe originally came from my Aunt Cecile Johnson; however, we adopted it as our family recipe years ago.*

## Ingredients

| | |
|---|---|
| 2 | sticks butter, softened |
| 2 | cups granulated sugar |
| 4 | large eggs |
| 1½ | cups flour |
| 6 | tablespoons unsweetened cocoa |
| 2 | tablespoons vanilla extract |
| 2 | cups pecan pieces |

Preheat oven to 350°F

**1.** Cream butter and sugar. Add eggs one at a time, and blend.

**2.** Sift flour and cocoa together and add to butter mixture. Add 1 cup of nuts. Pour into greased 9 x 13 baking dish, top with remaining cup of nuts, and bake approximately 30 minutes.

**To serve:** Serve with vanilla ice cream and caramel sauce.

*Chef's secret: 1 teaspoon of orange extract can be substituted for vanilla.*

## Shopping List

butter
granulated sugar
eggs
all-purpose flour
unsweetened cocoa
vanilla extract
pecan pieces

# Donald's Tangy Lemon Bars

Yields 2 dozen bars

*My friend and talented pastry chef Donald James shares this fool-proof recipe for these tasty bars.*

## Ingredients

### Crust
2 cups all-purpose flour
¾ cup butter, softened
¾ cup sugar

### Filling
4 eggs
2 cups sugar
2 teaspoons grated lemon peel
⅛ teaspoon salt

¼ cup lemon juice
¼ cup flour
1 teaspoon baking powder

### Glaze
1 cup powdered sugar
1 tablespoon butter
2 tablespoons lemon juice (or a little less)

Preheat oven to 350°F

**1.** In a 3-quart mixing bowl, combine crust ingredients. Mix at medium speed, scraping sides of bowl, 2-3 minutes or until well mixed and particles are fine. Pat into ungreased 13 x 9-inch pan.

**2.** Bake crust near center of oven for 18-22 minutes until very light brown.

**3.** Meanwhile, in the same bowl, combine eggs, sugar, lemon peel, salt, and lemon juice. Blend 1-2 minutes until well blended. Add flour and baking powder, blending well.

**4.** Pour filling into hot crust; return to oven and bake 23-25 minutes until top is golden brown.

**5.** Mix all glaze ingredients and pour over bar mixture when completely cool.

**To serve:** Serve with jasmine tea for an afternoon treat.

**Chef's secret:** *½ cup of coconut can be added to the filling for extra flavor.*

## Shopping List

| | |
|---|---|
| all-purpose flour | salt |
| butter | lemon juice |
| sugar | baking powder |
| eggs | powdered sugar |
| lemon peel | |

# Mini Pecan Tassies

Yields 48

*My mother has made these so often through the years, she needs no written recipe. They appear on every sweet table for holidays, weddings, and other special times.*

## Ingredients

**Crust**

| | |
|---|---|
| 1 | pound cream cheese, softened |
| 2 | cups (1 pound) butter, unsalted |
| 4 | cups flour |
| ¼ | teaspoon salt |

**Filling**

| | |
|---|---|
| 3 | tablespoons butter, melted |
| 3 | eggs |
| 2½ | cups light brown sugar |
| 1 | teaspoon salt |
| 1 | teaspoon almond extract |
| 1½ | cups chopped pecans |
| | Powdered sugar for dusting |

Preheat oven to 350°F

**Crust:**

**1.** For the crust, cube cream cheese and butter and place in a mixer or larger bowl. Beat to combine well. Add flour and salt, mixing a little in at a time. Form into ball and chill for at least one hour.

**2.** Form dough into 1-inch balls. Press balls into mini muffin tins to form shells. Keep chilled while mixing filling.

### Filling:

**1.** Combine butter, eggs, brown sugar, salt, and almond extract. Add pecans. Fill each chilled shell with about 1 teaspoon of filling.

**2.** Bake at 350°F for 25-30 minutes until filling has risen and set. Let cool and remove to rack for further cooling. Before serving, dust with powdered sugar.

**To serve:** Serve with a strong French roast coffee.

**Chef's secret:** *These freeze great!*

### Shopping List

| | |
|---|---|
| cream cheese | light brown sugar |
| butter | almond extract |
| flour | pecans |
| salt | powdered sugar |
| eggs | |

# Brown Sugar Praline Bars

Yields 24 bars

*This recipe is from my good friend Joan Strandlie.*

## Ingredients

1½ cups flour
1¼ cups brown sugar
1 egg
⅓ cup butter, softened
2 tablespoons milk
1 teaspoon baking powder
1 teaspoon almond extract
¼ teaspoon salt
½ cup broken pecan pieces

**Brown Sugar Glaze**
½ cup brown sugar
2 tablespoons butter
1 tablespoon milk
½ cup powdered sugar

Preheat oven to 350°F

**1.** Combine all ingredients except nuts. Beat in mixer at medium speed for 1 minute.

**2.** Spread in 9 x 13-inch casserole pan. Sprinkle with pecans, bake at 350°F for 25-30 minutes. Cool and drizzle with glaze.

**Brown Sugar Glaze:**

Yields approximately 1 cup

**1.** Melt brown sugar, butter, and milk together.

**2.** Stir in powdered sugar and drizzle over cooled bars.

## Shopping List

flour
brown sugar
eggs
butter
milk
baking powder
almond extract
salt
pecan pieces
powdered sugar

# Cocoons

Yields 4-5 dozen cookies

Mother had an Italian friend we called Miz Camille, who would get together with my mother and make the most delicious cookies for holidays and family gatherings. Cocoons were one of those items they used to make in large batches. I can recall that heavenly smell and eating the ones that didn't make the first cut. My job was to help with the rolling in powdered sugar. When I moved to Texas, this cookie not only took a different shape, but the name changed to Mexican Wedding Cakes. In the Latin culture, these are made traditionally for weddings. Cocoon refers to the shape of the cookie.

## Ingredients

| | |
|---|---|
| 2 | sticks butter |
| ¾ | cup powdered sugar |
| 2 | teaspoons almond extract |
| 2 | cups all-purpose flour |
| 1 | cup pecan pieces |
| 1 | cup powdered sugar for rolling |

Preheat oven to 325°F

**1.** Cream butter and powdered sugar; beat in almond extract. Gradually add flour and mix in pecan pieces. Wrap and chill dough at least one hour.

**2.** Cut and shape dough into cylinders (about 1½ inches long) like cocoons and place on an ungreased cookie sheet.

**3.** Bake for 25 minutes at 325°F. Let cool and roll in powdered sugar.

**To serve:** Serve with jasmine tea for an afternoon get-together.

**Chef's secret:** *This cookie freezes very well; bake and place in airtight bag.*

## Shopping List

butter
powdered sugar
almond extract
all-purpose flour
pecan pieces

# Classic Pecan Pralines

### Yields 3-4 dozen

*Two things that Louisiana has plenty of are pecans and sugar. Pralines have always been a big seller for the tourists; they just can't resist that sweet snack sold by the street vendors.*

*A candy thermometer is a must for successful pralines.*

### Ingredients

| | |
|---|---|
| 1 | cup packed light brown sugar |
| 1 | cup granulated sugar |
| ½ | cup heavy cream |
| 2 | tablespoons butter |
| 1 | teaspoon vanilla |
| 2 | cups pecans |

Stove top

**1.** Mix sugars and heavy cream in a heavy saucepan and cook over medium heat until it reaches soft ball stage (240°F). Remove from heat and add butter, stirring, then add vanilla.

**2.** Beat with a wooden spoon until the shine is gone and it has cooled slightly.

**3.** When the mixture starts to thicken, add pecans, mix well, and drop by spoonfuls on parchment paper or waxed paper.

**To serve:** Serve with café au lait for a quick pick-me-up.

*Chef's secret: The secret to making good pralines is knowing when to take them off the heat. Candy will start to thread when ready. Coconut can also be added for flavor.*

### Shopping List

light brown sugar
granulated sugar
heavy cream
butter
vanilla
pecans

# Brandy Torched Bananas

Serves 4

## Ingredients

4 large ripe bananas
1 tablespoon lemon juice
2 tablespoons melted butter
¼ cup brown sugar
½ teaspoon cinnamon
¼ teaspoon nutmeg
Splash of brandy
¼ cup heavy cream
Toasted coconut for garnish

Stove top

**1.** Peel bananas; cut in half lengthwise. Sprinkle with lemon juice.

**2.** In a large skillet, mix melted butter and brown sugar; cook for 5 minutes.

**3.** Add seasonings and bananas. Splash on brandy and ignite. Pour in heavy cream after flame is down and cook for 3-5 minutes. Serve hot. Garnish with toasted coconut.

**To serve:** Serve with French roast coffee and chicory and banana liqueur.

*Chef's secret: Always use extreme caution when lighting liqueurs; it is best to use fireplace matches for safe results.*

## Shopping List

bananas
lemon juice
butter
brown sugar
cinnamon
nutmeg
brandy
heavy cream
coconut

# Skillet Pineapple Upside-Down Cake

Yields 8-10 servings

*In the middle 1700s the West Indies introduced pineapples to the Deep South. It is said that the first recipe for Pineapple Upside-down Cake came from a cannery. This is a great bottoms-up dessert that can made with pantry ingredients on hand.*

## Ingredients

| | |
|---|---|
| 4 tablespoons butter | ⅔ cup granulated sugar |
| ½ cup dark brown sugar, packed | 1 large egg |
| 1 20-ounce can sliced pineapple, drained | 1¼ cups all-purpose flour |
| | 2 teaspoons baking powder |
| 10 pecan halves | ½ teaspoon salt |
| 4 tablespoons butter flavored shortening | ½ cup buttermilk |
| 2 teaspoons grated lemon rind | 1 teaspoon pineapple or lemon extract |

Preheat oven to 350°F

**1.** Melt butter in a 10-inch cast iron skillet. Sprinkle brown sugar evenly over butter and cook for 3 minutes, stirring occasionally.

**2.** Arrange pineapple slices on butter and sugar mixture, cutting pineapple if needed.

**3.** Place a pecan in the center of each pineapple ring and in other spaces; set aside.

**4.** Combine shortening and lemon rind, mixing well. Gradually add sugar, beating until light and fluffy. Add egg; beat well.

**5.** Combine dry ingredients. Mix into creamed mixture, alternating with the buttermilk. Stir in extract.

**6.** Spoon batter over pineapple slices in prepared skillet. Bake at 350ºF for 35-45 minutes or until toothpick comes out clean. Cool 10 minutes and invert cake to serving plate.

**To serve:** Serve with whipped cream.

*Chef's secret: Canned apricots and peaches work well as an upside-down cake also.*

### Shopping List

| | |
|---|---|
| butter | eggs |
| dark brown sugar | all-purpose flour |
| canned sliced pineapple | baking powder |
| pecan halves | salt |
| butter flavored shortening | buttermilk |
| lemon rind | pineapple or lemon extract |
| granulated sugar | |

# Quick Pecan Trifle

Yields approximately 20 servings

*Although trifle is not historically a Cajun dish, it is much loved throughout the South. Roasted pecans give this one a Louisiana touch. It's great for a take-along dessert.*

## Ingredients

| | |
|---|---|
| 2 | cups pecans |
| 2 | frozen pound cakes, thawed |
| 1 | 16-ounce jar caramel butterscotch topping |
| 2 | 3-ounce packages white chocolate pudding mix |
| 6 | cups sweetened whipped cream (or non-dairy whipped topping in a pinch) |
| 2 | pints fresh blueberries |
| 1 | quart fresh strawberries |
| 4 | peaches, sliced |
| | Fresh mint for garnish |

Preheat oven to 350°F

**1.** Roast pecans on a cookie sheet at 350°F for 20 minutes. Let cool.

**2.** Slice pound cake into ½-inch slices. Spread caramel topping on each and place on a cookie sheet.

**3.** Make pudding according to package directions. Set aside to "set up."

**4.** Whip cream; set aside. Wash berries and set aside.

**5.** Assemble in a clear large bowl or casserole dish (about 3-quart size) in the following order: 1/2 cup pecans, 2 cups pudding, 1/4 of the cake slices, blueberries, 1½

cups whipped cream. Repeat with remaining fruits in the same order. Top with fresh mint.

**To serve:** Serve with a rich dark French roast coffee.

*Chef's secret: Angel food cake and yogurt can be substituted for pound cake and whipped cream for a lighter dish.*

## Shopping List

pecans

frozen pound cakes

caramel butterscotch topping

white chocolate pudding mix

whipped cream or non-dairy
 whipped topping

fresh blueberries

fresh strawberries

fresh peaches

fresh mint

# Beverages

Legend has it that the cocktail was invented in New Orleans by an apothecary named A.A. Peychaud, when he started adding his famous bitter recipe to brandy. Libations have become a part of the rites of passage for many young party animals. The doors of the famous Pat O' Brian's can attest to this. This institution is in the French Quarter and is quite spectacular. When you enter, you walk through a long breezeway and enter onto a large patio with fountains and palm trees. The atmosphere is festive, and they do their best to make your visit memorable. This is what makes "the city that care forgot" so colorful.

# The Sazerac

### Serves 1

There is a famous Sazerac Lounge in the Fairmount Hotel in New Orleans that serves an authentic version of this cocktail. Sure to cure what ails you. Even if you don't know what it is.

### Ingredients

1   lump sugar
1   dash Angostura bitters
1   jigger rye whiskey
1   dash absinthe substitute
1   slice lemon peel

Directions:

Mix well and pour over cracked ice.

### Shopping List

cubed sugar
Angostura bitters
rye whiskey
absinthe substitute or Pernod
lemon peel

# Brandy Milk Punch

### Serves 6

### Ingredients

1   cup milk
¾   cup brandy
1   cup half-and-half cream
2   tablespoons superfine sugar
1   tablespoon vanilla extract
Ice cubes
Freshly grated nutmeg for
    garnish

Directions:

Mix all ingredients in a blender.

**Chef's secret:** *To make superfine sugar, place granulated sugar in a food processor and process for one minute.*

### Shopping List

milk
brandy
half-and-half cream
superfine sugar
vanilla extract
nutmeg

# Mint Julep

## Serves 1

*Silver cups are "de rigeur" for these tasty drinks. A hand ice crusher makes a big difference in the taste. For those hot afternoons, be sure and chill the cups before serving.*

### Ingredients

5-7 mint leaves plus some for garnish
1 teaspoon superfine or powdered sugar
1 tablespoon water or more
2½ tablespoons bourbon whiskey
Crushed ice

### Directions:

Crush mint leaves; add sugar and water. Add bourbon and pour over crushed ice. Garnish with extra mint sprigs.

### Shopping List

fresh mint leaves
superfine or powdered confectioner's sugar
bourbon whiskey
crushed ice

# Café Au Lait

## Yields 2 cups

*Children of all ages love this drink. When we were little, Mama gave us this instead of coffee. Chicory was imported to stretch coffee during Napoleonic times. The practice stayed and became part of the culture.*

### Ingredients

1 cup hot milk
1 cup of coffee and chicory (New Orleans blend)
Sugar if desired

### Directions:

Pour hot (*not* boiling) milk and coffee in the cup at the same time. Add sugar if needed.

### Shopping List

milk
coffee and chicory blend
sugar

# French 75

### Serves 1

*Here is the perfect drink for a celebration toast.*

### Ingredients

1   jigger brandy
Lemon juice
Champagne

Directions:

Pour brandy in a champagne glass, add a splash of lemon juice, and top with champagne.

### Shopping List

brandy
lemon juice
champagne


# Cajun Martini

### Serves 1

*These taste best served in a mason jar that's chilled.*

### Ingredients

2   ounces premium vodka or gin
Dash of dry vermouth
1   pickled jalapeño or cayenne pepper
Lemon twist

Directions:

Prepare as a regular martini, and if you are really feeling brave, use a little jalapeno juice or cayenne powder to make it "dirty."

### Shopping List

premium vodka or gin
dry vermouth
pickled jalapeño or cayenne pepper
lemon

# Martin's Bloodies

### Makes 4 drinks

*M*y husband, Martin, has a real talent for concocting fantastic Bloody Marys. It is one of his most-requested drinks at parties. He shares the recipe that he has developed to perfection over the years.

## Ingredients

4   jiggers of gin or vodka
1   quart of Clamato juice
Dash of pickle juice
Dash of Worcestershire sauce
Dash of Tabasco
Dash of celery salt
Dash of cayenne pepper
Dash of seasoned salt
Dash of lemon pepper
Pinch of dill weed
Juice of one lime
4   pickle spears
12  olives

Directions:

Mix ingredients and stir. Garnish with pickles and olives.

Serve with a "snit," which is a side of beer.

## Shopping List

gin or vodka
Clamato juice
pickles and juice
Worcestershire sauce
Tabasco
celery salt
cayenne pepper
seasoned salt
lemon pepper
dill weed
lime juice
olives

# Party Punch for a Crowd

### Serves 50

This is a light, refreshing punch that is perfect for large parties such as weddings.

### Ingredients

2  quarts lemonade
2  quarts pineapple juice
2  quarts orange juice
2  quarts ginger ale (use 3 if not using champagne)
1  bottle champagne (optional)
Fresh strawberries and mint for garnish

Directions:

**1.** Mix all juices; reserve some to make an ice ring with and freeze.

**2.** Add ginger ale and champagne right before serving.

### Shopping List

lemonade
pineapple juice
orange juice
ginger ale
champagne
fresh strawberries
fresh mint

# Hurricane Punch

### Serves 1

Although the original recipe for this punch is a closely guarded secret, there is always speculation as to who has managed to almost perfectly duplicate it. This may well be the one.

### Ingredients

1  jigger dark rum
1  jigger light rum
1  jigger grenadine
1  ounce orange juice
1  splash lime juice
1  splash pineapple juice

Directions:

Mix rums, grenadine, and orange juice. Top with lime and pineapple juices.

### Shopping List

dark rum
light rum
grenadine
orange juice
lime juice
pineapple juice

# Plantation Punch

Serves 1

### Ingredients

1    ounce dark rum
½    ounce grenadine
2    ounces orange juice
Splash of lemon juice
Ginger ale

Directions:

Mix all ingredients; top with ginger ale.

### Shopping List

dark rum
grenadine
orange juice
lemon juice
ginger ale

# Tropical Holiday Punch

Yields 3 quarts

*T*his punch is easy to make and tastes great. Make an ice ring out of orange juice for a contrast in color.

### Ingredients

1    envelope of unsweetened drink mix (your favorite flavor)
1    cup sugar
2    cups ginger ale
2    cups pineapple juice
¼    cup lime juice
2    quarts water

Directions:

Combine ingredients just before serving.

**To serve:** Serve with fresh mint floating on top as a garnish.

***Chef's secret:*** *Ice cubes made from this punch are great with iced tea.*

### Shopping List

unsweetened drink mix (any flavor)
sugar
ginger ale
pineapple juice
lime juice

# Scarlett Mocktail

Yields 1 serving

### Ingredients

4 ounces cran-raspberry juice
½ ounce sweet and sour mix
3 ounces sparkling mineral water
1 ounce orange juice
Ice cubes as needed

Directions:

Pour cran-raspberry juice and sweet and sour mix over ice. Add sparkling mineral water and top with orange juice.

### Shopping List

cran-raspberry juice
sweet and sour mix
sparkling mineral water
orange juice

# Carnival Punch

Yields 3 quarts

*This drink is popular at Mardi Gras. You may add rum for a little extra kick.*

### Ingredients

2 46-ounce cans pineapple juice
2 10-ounce packages frozen strawberries
1 6-ounce can white lemonade
¼ cup grenadine syrup
1 quart ginger ale
Lime slices for garnish
Fresh mint for garnish

Directions:

Combine all ingredients; garnish with lime and mint.

**To serve:** Serve with spiced nuts.

### Shopping List

pineapple juice
frozen strawberries
white lemonade
grenadine syrup
ginger ale
lime
fresh mint

# Zurracapote

Yields 4-6 servings (about 1 quart)

*This spicy beverage comes from the Spanish influence in New Orleans.*

## Ingredients

1   bottle dry red wine
⅓   cup sugar
1   cup mulling spices (tied in a cheesecloth)
Peel of one orange
½   cup Spanish brandy or port

Stove top or crock pot

Mix all ingredients and place in a crock pot. Heat for 2 hours on low.

**To serve:** Serve with bits of apple slices as garnish.

***Chef's secret:*** *This can also be used as a terrific poaching liquid for fruit.*

## Shopping List

dry red wine
sugar
mulling spices
orange
Spanish brandy or port

# Festive Raspberry Hot Chocolate

## Yields 4 servings

*Hot white chocolate is delicious for a chilly December Sunday afternoon when friends stop by for some holiday cheer.*

### Ingredients

4   ounces white baking chocolate, chopped

⅔   cups brewed coffee

3   cups milk or light cream

1   teaspoon raspberry flavored syrup

Ground cinnamon and nutmeg

Stove top

**1.** In a small saucepan over very low heat, melt white chocolate. Stir in coffee and mix well, heating until smooth.

**2.** Add cream and heat until hot, being careful not to scald the mixture.

**3.** Remove from heat and pour in blender. Blend until frothy, pour into mugs, and sprinkle with cinnamon and nutmeg.

**To serve:** Serve with a tray of sweets.

***Chef's secret:*** *Chambord liqueur can be added.*

### Shopping List

white chocolate baking bar

coffee

milk or light cream

raspberry flavored syrup

cinnamon

nutmeg

# *Index*

## Contacts for Louisiana Products:

Klieberts Alligator and Turtle Farm
41067 West Yellow Water Road
Hammond, LA 70403
504 / 345-3617
Alligator meat

Tony's Seafood Market
5215 Plank Road
Baton Rouge, LA 70805
504 / 357-9669
Crawfish, seafood, and seasonings

Louisiana Crawfish Company
140 Russell Cemetery Coad
Natchitoches, LA 71457
toll free 888 / 522-7292
e-mail: jd@lacrawfish.com
Crawfish, alligator, boudin and andouille sausage,
and Louisiana spices

Magic Seasonings Mail Order
P.O. Box 23342
New Orleans, LA 70183-0342
800 / 457-2857
web site: www.chefpaul.com
Tasso ham, andouille sausage, Cajun spices, and
other good things for good cooks

You can call for a free listing of all Seafood Sources
in Louisiana from the Louisiana Seafood Promotions
Board at 504 / 568-5693.

A good web site is "Louisiana Food Sources."